In Sickness and in Health

A MEMOIR BY

Joclyn and Jeremy Krevat

꙰

For Jeremy, who held it together so I could.

For Joclyn, who taught me the meaning of bravery.

CONTENTS

Joclyn's Preface

I'd better go to the bathroom now since I won't be able to move for two hours. I am not about to use a bedpan. I reasoned this to myself as I struggled to get up. Jeremy had since left for the night to take care of Sedaris, our dog, and I was surprisingly short of breath. My "phew" surprised even the nursing assistant who stood in the room with me. "That was hard?" as I landed at the edge of my bed. I must have answered silently. Her worried eyes did not meet mine after that.

I was not left alone for the entire night. Dr. Bender entered and left several times, made adjustments to the intravenous lines in my arm, did not allow me to drink more than a few sips at a time, but I did manage to sleep a bit. He woke me up to tell me that I needed a procedure that would involve putting a balloon pump in through my groin to assist my heart.

My heart was not pumping enough blood to my organs. My kidneys had begun to fail. "Maybe that's why I can't pee." I think I really said that. Well, you should try. You won't be allowed to move after the procedure in case you start bleeding.

"What time is it?"

"Should I call your husband?"

"Yes, please."

"Hey, wait a second."

"Yes, Mrs. Krevat?"

"You know I'm only thirty-two, right? Do you think I'll be okay?"

"I do. But we need to do this now.

Jeremy's Preface

My stomach turned and it felt like someone had stuck their hand down through my throat and was squeezing with all their might as the ringing phone awakened me. When I had left the hospital my wife was uncomfortable but stable, if you can call a failing heart and constant vomiting for over 24 hours at the age of 32 uncomfortable but stable. According to Dr. Bender, the X-ray was not showing anything that bad, and the expert cardiologist we had just visited assumed her current symptoms were a reaction to her new heart medication. This news allowed me to return home to get some rest, wake up and pay the rent, and get the dog into dog care until our friends picked her up and took her to New Jersey for safekeeping while we worked out this unexpected, sudden drama in our lives. I just needed one night and a few hours of the morning to arrange my life so I could focus on my wife — whom I had just married six months earlier. As the ringing phone pierced my stomach with a pain I had never felt before, I knew a few more hours was probably asking too much. My life was about to take its second dramatic turn in a matter of ten days.

What made matters worse was the red alarm clock that read 4:02 a.m. I wished this was a bad dream from which I would awake, but I knew this was not going to happen. As much as I know there is no Santa Claus, no Tooth Fairy, and no chance for everlasting peace in the Middle East... this was no dream. Suddenly my stomach leapt from my body as I realized the voice on the other end of the phone might tell me that my wife was gone. The one thing I was certain of was that a call at 4:02 a.m. was not going to be good news. The 212 area code on the caller ID left little chance this was a drunk dial from my friend Sheila in Santa Monica. I picked up the phone, "Hullo???" Silence. Then, "Mr. Krevat? Your wife is experiencing complete heart failure. Her organs are shutting down and we need to insert a pump in her artery in an attempt to save her life. Do we have your approval to perform this procedure?"

CHAPTER 1

IN SICKNESS AND IN HEALTH

Joclyn

Seriously? The impression that the nurses do of me is a sullen, "This is so fucked up." It is; isn't it? The heart beating inside my body is not the one I was made with. I was born with a heart that has been sliced up and placed into slides; a pathologist wrote "Wow" underneath one of those slides, and maybe the rest is in the Hudson River. Seriously.

December 2, 2009. I can't stop throwing up, but I haven't eaten in over a day. Green effervescent bile comes up. This can't be good. "I think you are dying," Jeremy complains as I struggle into the car. I don't feel well. At. All. When Methodist Hospital sent me home on Thanksgiving, the Thursday before this day, I felt all right, considering that I had originally been admitted for "pneumonia" and discharged with "heart failure" — the news of which had been delivered in a bizarrely chipper fashion — "Oh, my God! You have SUCH a big heart failure!" Seriously. Methodist discharged me with a defibrillator vest called a "LifeVest" and besides it being really itchy and frightening, I thought I was going to be all right. Notwithstanding that the Vest was to be worn at all times except during a shower, and that its purpose was to deliver a shock (kindly euphemized as a "treatment") should I develop a heart arrhythmia which could lead to cardiac arrest. "Are you kidding me?" The news of this accouterment was delivered by the vendor, not by any medical professional, and he seemed pretty incensed that no one had told me that he was coming. I above the waist stripped for him and he stuck some electro-conductive pads on me and showed me how to operate it. I wasn't really listening, and imagined that I would pull it off and throw it on the floor if it ever started beeping or otherwise indicated that it was about to deliver a shock, but still, I undeniably viewed this as a gigantic inconvenience. Of course I would be all right. They sent me home on Thanksgiving, and I was thrilled to get the hell out of there. Hospitals are not all the same (I knew this already intuitively, but I also had just learned it firsthand) and I wouldn't recommend Methodist unless you happened to be standing in their Emergency Department already when someone happened to stab you. Go Anywhere Else, otherwise. Instructions given were to follow up in one week with a cardiologist. I made an appointment with a non-Methodist affiliated cardiologist recommended by my radiologist uncle. During the vomiting bile incident, we decided that seeing this Recommended Manhattan Doctor would be a better idea than going to the emergency room, Methodist or otherwise. Luckily, I'd brought a Ziploc container in which to vomit. When Fancy Cardiologist couldn't read my blood pressure, he suggested that I either come back the following day, or just go to Weill Cornell's emergency room so they could run all the necessary tests to really figure out what was going on.

Up until this doctor visit, I'd actually complained to best friend Charlene that the "LifeVest" was itchy. "It's itchy; I think I'll take it off."

"My ASS is itchy, Joclyn, but I still leave it there." That line, and "I'd almost rather be at work" were the two lines of comic relief often returned to throughout the course of this ordeal.

Given my ridiculous medical history, ripe with multiple autoimmune disorders, Jeremy and I instantly decided that going to the emergency room would be the smartest thing for us to do. Later, we realized that had we gone home, I may not have survived the night. I couldn't walk the block and a half to the emergency room entrance, so an ambulette was called. We would later receive an $800 bill for said ride. Yeah, right. Seriously.

After being tilted all the way back, the EMTs found that my blood pressure was 60/40. I waited in the emergency room, sticking my finger down my throat, convinced that I would begin to feel better if only I could throw up. "No, don't force it" some employee cautioned. What the fuck does she know, I wondered as I successfully vomited yet again.

(Weeks later, someone would tell me that excessive vomiting is a sign that the right side of the heart is failing. How peculiar, right?)

In the middle of the night, after I was situated in the cardiac intensive care unit, the wonderful Dr. Bender stood by. Checking, checking. I was sent to have a balloon put in to assist my heart. This somehow involved my groin, my femoral artery, and lots of lidocaine. I felt the balloon inside my chest. It was either making my heart beat very fast, or it had its own rhythm. I never asked. I thought it had worked.

Jeremy

When the phone woke me up a little after 4:00 a.m., I knew it was bad. There was really little hope that it was a wrong number, or a friend from California. Our friends don't have a habit of calling in the middle of the night, and few of them call our home landline phone. The truth is we never even gave out the house number. We do most of our phone business on our mobile phones; the house phone was just a bonus in our triple play package. I did give the number to the hospital because I did not want to keep my mobile phone on all night, sounding every time someone reached out to contact me via email, text, or Facebook chat. There was only one explanation for the phone ringing: it was the hospital, and something was happening to my wife that required calling me in the middle of the night. To this day, I have never felt more pain in my stomach than at the moment of that phone call. My eyes started to water and I felt like I was going to throw up. This call was not a dream. The alarm clock was blinking, and the 4:02 a.m. in red is an image that will probably always remain in my mind. This was the first moment I realized they might be calling me to tell me she was gone. I felt this could be the moment I lost everything. My hands were shaking.

When Dr. Bender told me that my wife was having kidney failure I was overcome with two strong feelings at the same time. The first was relief that she was alive, the second was shock. Kidney failure? Huh? Where did that come from? He quickly explained that Joclyn's heart failure prevented blood from reaching her organs. Her kidneys were the first to begin to shut down. I just started crying, and could not stop. I was no longer able to make sense of what was happening and the feeling of helplessness overcame me. As I worked to pull myself together and push away the thoughts of a funeral, and having to explain to all of our family and friends that Joclyn was gone for a mysterious reason nobody could explain, I took a deep breath and kept listening. Apparently they were planning to insert a balloon into an artery in Joclyn's leg that would help pump the blood to her organs. I could barely speak, but managed to whisper, "please tell my wife I love her." I hung up the phone and buried my head in my pillow, completely defeated. I kept asking myself how this could happen to someone like her. She did not deserve this or anything like it.

I married my wife on June 28th. The rabbi told us he hoped this would be the unhappiest day of the rest of our lives, and every other day would bring only more happiness. Aside from the Yankees sweeping the Mets in the first of two subway series in 2009, life was good. I was in the middle of a seven-week boot camp for the New York City Teaching Fellows. This is an accelerated program for people seeking to change careers and become teachers. It was not an easy program to get accepted into, and I felt lucky to sacrifice most of my summer for the opportunity.

Instead of leaving my career in technology and attending school full time to obtain a master's degree in education, this program offered a path that allowed me to become a teacher in just two months. This would be made possible by completing an intense eight-week summer program. In September, I would find a job in a local Brooklyn high school while earning my master's degree at night. This was a far better option than attending school for two years, while trying to earn money in some random job after 13 successful years in high tech sales and marketing. I ignored a lot of doubters who could not understand why I would take such a dramatic cut in pay to work with high school students in New York

City. It was something I had trouble explaining myself, I just wanted to teach. This was the price of following a calling that few understood.

Things were going well for my wife, Joclyn, as well. She was making very good money contracting at a nursing home as an occupational therapist. We had decided it was silly for her to work directly for a school or city hospital since contracting paid double, an interesting fact causing us to wonder why the city would pay so much more money to contractors, rather than just raise the pay scale for therapists. But it was no longer our concern; she became incorporated and my accountant helped her figure out all the wonderful benefits to being a contractor. This would make it possible for me to take that huge pay cut, and follow my dreams of making a difference for young people. Not long after the wedding I was interviewing for jobs and getting a taste for the monstrosity known to New Yorkers as the New York City Department of Education (NYCDOE). It was the same system I grew up in, only with a new name, and a lot more segregation than I ever remembered. One would never know Brown vs. the Board of Education had ever been settled. But that is another story.

After a challenging and busy summer preparing to be a teacher, the job hunt began. After a lot of interviews with no response or feedback, I went to a job fair at the new Citi Field and met my future boss. It was a perfect situation. The school was located a short drive away from our apartment, and I was hired as a 9th-grade teacher. As a teacher of children with special needs, I was to follow a group of 25–30 students to all of their classes. About ten of those students would be classified as students with special needs. This is the new environment created to meet the federal mandate for "free and appropriate education."

The new trend in special education called for special education students to be integrated into general education classrooms. There a team of two teachers — one of them licensed in special education — would serve their needs. This strategy allowed these students the social opportunities their peers received, and removed them from the isolation of the dedicated special education classroom. For some students, this is an ideal environment. The real challenge is making sure the right students are in the right environment. This is a much harder task than anyone could ever guess. It would allow me the opportunity to teach alongside four different teachers with more experience than I had. I thought it was a great opportunity to learn multiple teaching styles while I worked on finding ways to help my students succeed in their first year of high school. Meanwhile, Joclyn was doing well and providing a ray of sunshine for her patients that had little sunshine to speak of in their lives. I don't exaggerate when I say I married an angel.

One of the things Joclyn and I spent our extra time doing after work was jogging around Prospect Park. Joclyn loved it. Her enthusiasm and desire to run every evening was inspirational and maddening at the same time. I am by my nature a lazy human being. My preference was to come home and lie down and watch television. So many channels on cable, so much to watch. Joclyn would stare at me and practically put my running clothes on for me if it started to get too late. I always felt good after the run, and acted like I had no clue what she meant when she told me, "I told you so!"

All this jogging was quietly preparing my wife for something neither of us could ever have predicted. At the time it was just something Joclyn loved to do. In October, Joclyn signed up for a 10K that would take place right on our familiar running route in the park. I passed on the race because I was so busy at work and at graduate school in the evenings I had no time to train. So on a chilly Saturday afternoon I sat with our dog Sedaris and waited for Joclyn to come chugging past the finish line. Afterwards, Joclyn told me she could have kept running another mile or so and she felt great. She was in the best shape of her life, or at least felt like it.

October was a challenging month for me as I was only in my second month of teaching, and still learning the ropes in a very challenging environment. The days were long and made even longer by the graduate classes I was taking at City College. City College was over an hour away from the school by train and I often found myself running from work to the train in order to make it to class. There were days where I left for work by 6:30 a.m. and would not get back home until 10:30 p.m. The hardest part of that schedule was not being with Joclyn, as we were accustomed to eating dinner together and spending a lot of our free time with each other. Fortunately, my principal was happy with my work, and my co-teachers had yet to try to throw me out the window of the building. I was doing what I set out to do a couple of years earlier, and it would not have been possible without a supportive wife who encouraged me to place my happiness above finances. I married an angel, who turned out to be a saint as well.

Joclyn had a busy schedule too. Aside from her normal 9–5 job on Roosevelt Island, she was also contracting for the NYCDOE and working with pre-K children in need of occupational therapy. It was tiring for her to travel around Brooklyn to work these extra hours, but the money was great; we both have a taste for some of the finer things in life that are far from cheap. Joclyn felt it was worth the extra hours of work if it meant having more spending money for nice dinners, and lots of bottles of our favorite wines. When we finally had time together to relax, Joclyn loved to hear my stories from work. My new career certainly provided me with a lot of entertaining material. One of her favorites was about a student who traded information with me for good things to eat. I brought in a knish that I heated up in the morning for him to try. He loved it, and even added mustard following my recommendation. In exchange for introducing him to this new delicacy, he provided me with a new item to order from the deli, a toasted bagel with cream cheese and bacon. At first this took me by surprise, but then I thought about bacon just being a substitute for smoked salmon. It made sense since both were very salty as they were both smoked meat. Joclyn was excited to hear my review, which was very positive. I have eaten this concoction several times since, and am not ashamed to admit I love it!

As normal as life seemed to be, there was always a level of concern when it came to the health of my wife. Joclyn had a history of some autoimmune disorders that left her with inconveniences that made it hard to forget they had occurred. The first thing to note was that she had to have her colon removed eight years before we met. She actually had a "J-pouch" put in place of her colon. I had no idea what caused this; neither did I fully understand what it actually is, nor do I today as I write this. The one thing I knew was that it forced her to take medication that allowed her to avoid using the bathroom a dozen times a day. Instead, I have adjusted to her using the bathroom about five to six times on an average day. But the inconveniences do not end there. My wife has celiac disease. This means she cannot eat wheat gluten. This is not an easy thing to deal with when you live in the land of amazing pizza and bagels. I went from eating primarily in Italian restaurants to never eating in Italian restaurants. It is very hard to find a dish in an Italian restaurant that is not loaded with wheat in some form. While this was inconvenient, that's all it was — and giving up Italian restaurants for the sake of Joclyn's health was a tiny price to pay.

What really concerned me about Joclyn's health was her tendency to develop pneumonia. She had three bouts with pneumonia since we'd met a few years earlier. This had already landed her in the hospital, and the sight of her lying on a hospital bed was very unnerving. Joclyn is such a good person, and I felt she was the last person on earth who deserved to be ill. Illness is not something I would wish on my worst enemy. Having to watch my wife deal with it left me wishing I could jump in her place. Watching her suffer was far worse than going through it myself. I felt that I was stronger and that I could handle it better, a thought that is almost laughable to me now. Boy was I wrong. My other concern was that J-pouch in her body. I was worried that it would eventually cause a problem of some kind, so that anxiety never completely left my mind.

CHAPTER 2

SCRATCH MY BACK

Joclyn

Jeremy and I first met years ago, over the telephone. It was late 2002, and I was living in a residential part of Brooklyn called Mill Basin with Mo and Charlene. Mo and Jeremy had grown up next door to each other in Canarsie, Brooklyn where they both remained until early adulthood. I met Mo during my first semester in college, timed exactly with Jeremy's departure to California. We just missed each other, but Jeremy would call to speak to Mo often, and if Mo was not home, Jeremy and I would banter about common friends; he would do impressions and I would remark on his obvious talent as a mimic. I knew a little bit about Jeremy, as Mo would always refer to him in various connections. I placed Jeremy in the "facts about Mo" area of my memory.

We met in person, without realizing it, at Mo and Charlene's wedding in 2003. We were both in the bridal party, but I am pretty sure we didn't speak to each other directly. I definitely spoke to his date. In 2005 we met again at Mo's sister Liza's wedding, and realized after the fact that we were both part of the same conversation about the movie *Sideways*. Can you believe that merlot sales actually took a hit after that?

We met on purpose through the Internet in 2006. I was living in Washington, D.C. at that point and got a message on MySpace.

"I don't know if you remember me, but I thought I would say hi." Of course I remembered him.

"Of course I remember you. Those phone calls were the best part of that apartment!" That shared apartment in Brooklyn was pretty low-end. We emailed back and forth quite a lot and, while I regrettably deleted my MySpace account one day in a fit of something or other, I do still have the emails. As I was in the process of moving to a new apartment, and therefore lacked consistent Internet service, I probably heightened my appeal by not answering emails promptly. I inadvertently played hard to get.

Our MySpace and email banter quickly escalated to lengthy phone conversations of the kind that no one has anymore, the kind where you put the phone down on the counter and leave it on speaker while putting groceries away and cleaning up, or that you continue even though you are in a store buying your brother a football jersey for his 40th birthday.

I was planning a housewarming/New Year's Eve party at the new apartment, and I told Jeremy that he should come. I knew he wouldn't come, I told myself. He lived in California, was visiting family in North Carolina, and was planning on going to New York City for Christmas.

"I can't come; my friends in New York will kill me," turned into a rented car and a pickup from work one day (December 27th so just in case we didn't like each other, New Year's wouldn't be ruined) that had me so nervous that everyone at work knew even though I didn't want them to. I couldn't stop giggling and Jeremy and I stayed on the phone until I was actually opening the passenger side door of his rented car, hoping I was entering the correct car on the otherwise deserted roof of the hospital. The New Year's visit turned into an extended stay, a return visit a couple of weeks later, a gift of a trip for me to California the month after that, and a move-in date of April. Jeremy, this guy I met by accident and then on purpose was moving 3,000 miles to be with me.

"Shouldn't he get his own apartment?" someone asked.

I thought it was a little late for that. We were perfect for each other!

❧

It is hard to believe that was a whole heart ago. Even now, I can't even properly explain what it has been like. I feel inarticulate when people ask about it. It is like science fiction, and it can't possibly be something that actually happens to people, but it happened to me, and even as I sit in my in-laws' writing this, I am still justifiably terrified that it is not yet over. I am not attached to any crazy machines pumping blood external to my body, but every time I have a doctor's appointment I am faced with a very real threat of being readmitted to the hospital for any number of reasons. So far, I have been admitted for a "2R rejection," a "3B rejection," and a blood glucose level of 600. Oh, yeah. By the way, at some point it was decided that I also have either medically induced or Type 1 diabetes. That is not the adult-onset type. It is the autoimmune kind that typically first presents in childhood. So even though I am taking potently toxic immunosuppressant medication, I still apparently have the ability to develop new autoimmune diseases. I feel like the only ones I don't have are lupus and multiple sclerosis. I am terrified that those will be in the falling shoe. I shiver when I hear someone talk about medical conditions that seem especially life-altering, almost as though hearing about them will induce them. I probably need therapy, but in the meantime, I write.

Jeremy

When I first met Joclyn she appeared very healthy. Actually, I should say she sounded healthy. We did not actually meet in person. After graduating college I moved out to the Bay Area in California. Apparently my best friend and neighbor Mo found a replacement to accompany him to hang out in the parking lot of Edward's grocery store, Joclyn Gordon. Joclyn would later live with Mo and his girlfriend (and eventual wife) Charlene in Brooklyn. Whenever I would call to speak to Mo, Joclyn would answer the phone and we would talk, and usually poke fun at our mutual friends, as I have a habit of imitating those that I love. I would tell her funny stories about growing up next to Mo, and she would laugh while swearing that I was explaining so much. We never would have guessed or imagined that Mo and Charlene would be the best man and maid of honor at our wedding. That was actually years later and impossible to predict at that time.

Several years later after those conversations, I found myself visiting my parents for Thanksgiving in 2006. My brother Matthew and I were hanging out at his house just a couple of miles away from my parents' house. We were bored and Matthew asked me if I wanted to set up a MySpace page. I was planning on creating a page, and decided to take advantage of his willingness to type it up for me as I dictated my favorite TV shows, movies, and foods. As I began to look up and add friends to this page I used the common technique of adding a friend, and looking at their friends to find the ones I knew. When I looked at Mo's sister Liza's page, I saw the name "Joclyn Gordon." I remembered who she was but was not sure she would remember who I was, as it was at least five to six years since we spoke. Even as I was the best man at Mo's wedding, Joclyn was a bridesmaid and we did not even speak.

As my brother typed my dictated message to the friend request — "I am Mo's friend who used to speak with you on the phone when you lived with Mo and Charlene, do you remember?" — I was still unsure if she would accept. I was not familiar with social networking, and how happy people are to add friends. A few minutes later Joclyn responded, "Of course I remember you, that was the best part of living in that apartment." Matthew looked up at me and heartily exclaimed, "she wants you!"

When I returned to California our conversations over the Internet continued. Soon it was email, and eventually long phone calls. Since Joclyn was moving and without Internet, there were moments when I thought I scared her off. But when we did connect she insisted that she looked forward to speaking or chatting with me. During the Thanksgiving break Joclyn mentioned that she was throwing a housewarming party on New Year's Eve. I turned the offer down as that week was all about being back in New York and hanging with friends and feasting on my favorite foods. But now that it was mid-December and we were spending hours on the phone, I began to have second thoughts.

"Of course you are going down to D.C. to meet up with her, you idiot!" was the reaction of my close friend Sheila. We were sitting at our favorite wine bar in San Francisco and I had just finished giving her the Joclyn update. Sheila basically slapped some sense into me and reminded me that all I talked about is Joclyn, and how could I pass up the opportunity to visit her? Sheila explained that I would rent a car after Christmas and drive my sorry ass down to D.C. We did agree that I should go a few days before the new year in case it did not work out. That way I could make it back up to New York City for the new year if necessary.

A couple of weeks later I was in D.C. picking Joclyn up at work and I knew within minutes I would be spending the holiday with her. Even though Joclyn had already had some health issues, it never showed in the earlier days as we got to know each other. As a matter of fact, our relationship started out with me as the patient. While getting up from her low to the ground futon after watching some TV in the living room, I threw out my lower back. My back and I had a history of problems, but this was different. She convinced me to go to the emergency room. I worried Joclyn would realize what an old fart I was, but she was supportive and unfazed by the whole ordeal. I would celebrate that New Year very high on prescribed painkillers and muscle relaxers.

As I got to know Joclyn over the next few months, and she got to know me, we realized it was getting serious and decided one of us was going to have to move across the country. Luckily my manager had no issue with me working remotely, so I would not have to find a new job. After six months in the D.C. area, we both decided it was time to return to New York City. I was already thinking about becoming a teacher and I wanted to do it in New York. Joclyn was getting tired of her job, and realized she could make a lot more money contracting anyway. So, we found an apartment in Brooklyn, and I proposed to Joclyn on her birthday, somewhere between Bermuda and Florida on a Royal Caribbean Cruise ship. Everything was set.

While we lived in Brooklyn we had a great time planning our wedding and enjoying the beautiful neighborhood of Windsor Terrace. We were only minutes from Prospect Park and would take our dog Sedaris there every morning, as well as use the outer loop of the park to jog and keep in shape. Things got a little rough when Joclyn caught pneumonia and had to spend a few nights in the hospital. We almost did not go to the hospital, a decision that could have been deadly. That was a lesson that would pay off later on down the road. Joclyn had a second bout with pneumonia before our wedding. This only heightened my concern for her health.

Chapter 3

PAGING DR. HOUSE?

Jeremy

In spite of my concerns, in October of 2009 Joclyn was doing great. Her running had her in the best shape of her life and had people asking her for advice on how to stay so fit. That was the early part of October, and just a couple of weeks later she experienced a change. The first change was an unexplainable itch she kept complaining of. She would often ask me to scratch her back in the time that we had known each other, but she suddenly started demanding I scratch her back as she scratched the rest of her body. We both started to become concerned that she had contracted scabies at work. This was not a far-fetched suspicion as Joclyn worked in a rehabilitation nursing home with plenty of recovering drug addicts on Methadone. There had been a few scabies alerts, and Joclyn had even rubbed on some hormonal cream that was provided to her by her employers. The itching got worse, even after changing our laundry detergent to the non-allergenic variety. I started to develop an uneasy feeling. My wife was suffering and there was nothing I could do to help her.

After a couple of weeks, Joclyn started complaining that she felt out of breath; she even had to stop some of her jogs in the park after running only a few minutes. We felt she may have been working too hard and just needed some rest. We realized that working full time at the nursing home and providing occupational therapy services to children in the evening may have been too much. Before we got to test a plan of more relaxation Joclyn started to cough and seemed out of breath. I woke up one morning on the 18th of November and Joclyn looked up at me before I left for work and declared she was definitely sick and felt awful. She called in sick and got ready to go to the medical clinic near our apartment. We were both convinced it was pneumonia, and that would mean a week of antibiotics. Because Joclyn had been hospitalized a year earlier for pneumonia, we were determined to tend to it early if the symptoms resurfaced. I felt a little uneasy and was distracted at work; the image of my wife telling me she felt awful kept haunting me. I hated the thought of her being uncomfortable. My inability to help her was even harder for me to accept.

It didn't surprise me when Joclyn texted me to pick up her prescription on my way home from work. I was relieved that the doctor must have agreed a round of antibiotics would have her back to normal by the end of the week. It was Wednesday and Thanksgiving was only eight days away. Plenty of time for a full recovery and dinner in Edgewater, New Jersey with the Goldners that included Mo's parents Eileen and Stanley as well as Liza's family, and of course Mo and Charlene. During the year, their rock band "Spanking Charlene" and full-time jobs keep them tremendously busy. So this was time we all looked forward to spending together and never took for granted. The only problem was that on Saturday morning there was no denying that Joclyn was not feeling any better. She was really having difficulty breathing, and I went into my crazy Jewish panic mode. It was time to step up our level of treatment and see Dr. Din. This was a doctor in Park Slope, Brooklyn that had earned our trust during Joclyn's last bout with pneumonia. To my embarrassment and chagrin, Joclyn went right out to the car in her pajamas. My disparagement is something she still haunts me with today. I thought at the time that if she showed up like that, they would think we did not have insurance. Or at least that was my justification for my temporary insanity, a condition that would show its face again as my anxiety continued to heighten, clouding my better judgment.

When Dr. Din was deciding if Joclyn should go home with a new prescription, Joclyn remarked that she hoped going home would not end up being a fatal decision. He thought about it for a few seconds more and called the hospital to arrange an X-ray of her chest. We walked to the hospital because the car was parked in a spot that was as close to the hospital as we were going to get. We were emotionally preparing for three days of inconvenience and frustration in the hospital. We both had a feeling they were not going to let us go right home. We had been through this before and knew it was never fun to be stuck in a hospital for any amount of time. At the same time, I was relieved we were going to the hospital; Joclyn's breathing was getting worse and she appeared out of breath. I wanted them to get those meds into her as soon as possible. While we were in the waiting room in the back, after a wait in the first waiting area, a nurse shared my concern and hooked her up to a breathing machine that I usually see kids with asthma use to help clear their lungs. It seemed to help her, but she was still struggling to breathe. After a couple of hours, the emergency room staff took an X-ray of Joclyn's chest, and, a couple of hours after that, they announced that fluid in both sides of her lungs blocked their ability to diagnosis her. The best guess was still pneumonia. A short stay in the hospital to make sure was recommended. The emergency room staff was confident we would be home by Thanksgiving.

Unlike the year before, Joclyn would not have her own room. Her elder roommate was very quiet, but had many guests that were never quiet. What made it worse was that Joclyn does not speak Spanish, so she could not even look for entertainment in the context of all the conversations. Sharing a bathroom with a stranger is never much of a picnic either. I kept promising Joclyn it was only for a few days and that we would be home soon. She was getting the medicine we thought would certainly start having her better by the following day. I felt as though someone had given me a soft punch to the gut when Joclyn was still short of breath the next day. I kept asking her if there was any improvement, and she finally snapped at me and yelled, "I don't know, I can't tell, stop asking!" This was a clear indication she was not getting better. The doctors started trying different treatments as well. We were far from pleased when they started loading her up with steroids. I joked that if she was a major league baseball player she would not be able to pass a drug test. She smiled politely. Humor is my way of dealing with almost all situations, but this situation seemed to be getting more critical as we hit the third day with no improvement. The newest delivery of news was there seemed to be some fluid near her heart. The doctors were admittedly uncertain of what was going on. This was beginning to feel like an episode of *House*.

Joclyn

Thinking that I'd come down with pneumonia for the third time in two years, I stayed home from work one day and took myself to the walk-in clinic just a few blocks away from our street-level row-house apartment in Windsor Terrace. The walk was difficult, a struggle, actually, but hey, pneumonia changes your breathing. So that must have been what was going on, I reasoned with myself and thus did not panic.

I sat in the waiting room with all of the other people with minor illnesses. Being the wife of someone who had just become a New York City public school teacher only two months prior meant that, naturally, our health insurance cards had not yet arrived, although I did happen to know that we were technically covered as of the first day of school. Rather than argue with the receptionist who'd only made me wait just over an hour to be seen, I paid the $50 fee for uninsured people and went in to be examined. Explaining my respiratory theory must have been convincing, and my mention of how I had been so incredibly itchy lately, and that, because I worked in a nursing home that had recently experienced a scabies outbreak I also thought that I might possibly have or have had the disgusting body hair infestation was met with a cursory skin inspection and a chuckle. I had, after all, doused myself in the prophylactic (and toxic) skin cream just days earlier. A pesticide, yes. A prescription for Avelox and a chest X-ray later, I headed over to the pharmacy. I did not get the chest X-ray, but I dutifully took the antibiotics. On Saturday morning, three days later, I was surprised to feel that the antibiotics had not done a thing. Strange, since generally I would have been feeling much better, at least on an upswing that I'd notice, in any event. I was pretty sure that I was feeling worse, scarily. Just walking from the recliner chair in the living room to the kitchen, one room over, for a drink, made me plop back down, slightly short of breath, with a "Whoo! That was hard!"

"Really?" Jeremy wondered, asking more than once.

We dragged me to the neighborhood's other walk-in clinic, the one that kept weekend hours, and which also happened to be the one also familiar with my recent medical history. Jeremy was not thrilled that I had no intention of getting dressed, and that I thought it just fine to attend a doctor's office in pajamas, particularly when I was feeling like crap. Dr. Din said my best bet would be to go the Emergency Department for a chest X-ray, since that would be the fastest way to get one done and have it read, since it was a Saturday.

I found myself seated in the asthma section of triage, finally, after having dealt with the main waiting room filled with children, none of whom appeared ill; they seemed content and playful, rather, and yet their parents had all seemingly conspired on the sign-in sheet and all written that the reason for visiting the hospital was "chest pain." A fine trick, that is, because "chest pain" triggers priority attention for the complainant. If everyone complains of chest pain, of course, then the overall wait time for each person remains unchanged, except, of course, mine, since I was not experiencing chest pain. It would turn out that I was experiencing heart failure, and really should have been seen first, but why would I have thought that shortness of breath and generalized chest discomfort — that I didn't even think about until after the fact (really, it was not until weeks later that I would remember having to let everyone go in front of me up the subway steps after adjusting the strap on my messenger bag so it was not directly across the center of my chest) — would mean something so ridiculously dire?

Following intake and a vital signs reading, I am attached to a nebulizer to help with my breathing, and eventually have a chest X-ray to look for fluid in my lungs. There is not much urgency to either of these procedures, and I'm mostly annoyed, just wishing to be hooked to intravenous antibiotics already.

I had suspected on traveling to the emergency room that I would somehow be admitted to the hospital for at least an overnight stay, so when I was told that I was being admitted based on the result of my chest X-ray, I was again annoyed, but hardly taken aback. "There is a lot of fluid in your lungs, but it's hard to tell where it is all coming from" is what I seem to remember hearing. How did that not send Jeremy and I into a panic? Well, no one seemed that concerned, really. A doctor may have also explained to us that the entire "field" was not visible in the X-ray as well, or something as incomprehensible as that.

Following admission, I settled into a hospital room with a farter. Someone fancied it a fine idea to house me with an older woman who had lots wrong with her, and who also had frequent multitudes of loud visitors occupying all of the chairs and horning in on my curtained area. Her most common visitor was a teenager who seemed to be her granddaughter. While grandma napped and farted, grandchild screamed into a cell phone and laughed and ate. Normally, of course, I am not so critical and insensitive. Being in the hospital had taken a toll on me, given my medical history and apparent confusion about what was wrong with me. In my healthy, outside of the hospital life, I would have viewed my neighbor and guests as a typical family with all the humorous quirks of any family.

I dozed and zoned and waited for Jeremy to arrive, all the while noticing that the intravenous antibiotics to which I was plugged did not seem to be making me feel any better. My veins throbbed at times, and the IV lines needed to be adjusted. It was as though I was dehydrated while also attached to fluids. And so went Friday, Saturday, Sunday, and most of Monday. Uneventful, yet somewhat appalling. When would I start to feel better? At some point over the weekend, I showered. I was feeling weak, and so Jeremy stayed right by the bathroom door. This was in case I needed assistance, but it was also to keep the farter and her family away. Jeremy looked worried, and I just continued to not understand what was going on. I realized aloud that I had not used the bathroom in a long time. This was quite unusual for me. Jeremy really looked worried.

CHAPTER 4

YOU CAN'T BE TALKING TO ME?!

Jeremy

It was 5:30 p.m. on a Monday evening just three days before Thanksgiving. We checked into the hospital on Saturday and the doctors had decided to run an echocardiogram on Joclyn. As I looked on over the shoulder of the nurse taking pictures of the image of my wife's heart, I remarked how her heart looked like a little mouse struggling to keep up with the rest of the litter. It just looked like it was pumping really fast in a panic, but not accomplishing much. Then again, my heart may look exactly the same. I know nothing about organs and what they are supposed to look like in live video. When the test was over a doctor came in and told us Joclyn could have an issue with swelling in her heart; that was the most probable cause of the fluids in her lower lungs. He assured us the staff was confident it was a virus and she would ride it out and be fine. In the meantime Joclyn would take Lasix. We were told Lasix would help drain the fluids from her lungs and heart to help her breathing. He was right about the Lasix. Taking Lasix, Joclyn urinated enough to fill the fuel tank of Willie Nelson's bus, which runs on alternative energy. The effect of Lasix on Joclyn was easier and more comfortable breathing. We were happy about what was happening and even joking around when suddenly a young Asian female entered the room and casually said (in a California valley girl way), "Oh my god! You have such a big heart failure!"

I do not know what it is like to have somebody swing a baseball bat directly into my stomach, but I do not think it would cause me as much abdominal pain as I was feeling at this moment in my life. Gasping for air we both tried to convince this woman that she was speaking to the wrong patient. The doctor just told us she would be fine. The lady must have just then realized the gravity of the situation for the first time, because her facial expression changed as we began to turn white as ghosts. She nervously explained that some number that represents the strength in which the heart pumps blood is a 10, and that the normal output is 50. Joclyn kept insisting that she felt fine and this was a mistake. I started hyperventilating and feeling that our lives were never going to be the same. Suddenly several doctors came into the room and told us they were moving Joclyn upstairs to the Cardiology Department. As they wheeled her up, Joclyn kept asking if she was going to be all right. We were getting mixed responses that always included the information that her heart had taken a lot of damage. The doctors insisted that she was having heart failure. I was crying inside. I was devastated. I found myself wishing I could wake up from this nightmare, but I kept telling Joclyn that everything was going to be all right.

After a few hours of settling into our new dwelling, not much was happening. Doctors would occasionally come in to provide new information, which in our state of mind just confused us more. It was about midnight; I was passing out when we both agreed I should go home and get some sleep. It was going to be a long ride ahead, and we decided that I was going to have to treat this situation like a marathon runner. This meant conserving energy and not burning myself out before it was over, let alone before it had really started. I learned that while many people think you need to be there every minute of the day for your loved one in the hospital, you take a great risk if you burn out and are not strong enough to help them all the way until the end. I was determined to see this through, and the plan was to remember to take care of myself, so I could take care of Joclyn. As I walked home I texted the names of the stores I was passing on the way. Joclyn loved this information and insisted I keep doing it until the moment I got to the front door. Joclyn also insisted I describe the reaction of Sedaris (our dog) when I walked through the door. Joclyn and I then spent a few minutes texting each other apologies for all the thoughtless things we ever said or did to each other, and how much we loved one another. After walking Sedaris, I went to bed trying not to imagine or think about the possibility of being alone like this permanently. Under the circumstances, this was no small effort. Joclyn was fighting for her life, and I was no longer sure it was a fight she was going to win.

The next day I returned to work. As a first-year teacher I could not take too many days off, and I needed to conserve them considering we did not know what lay ahead. I started to think about what would happen if Joclyn did not make it through this and I lost her. I was so convinced her life was in jeopardy I even sent an email to a longtime friend of Joclyn's that we had a falling out with after our wedding. I felt it would be wrong to have her and her husband find out she passed away after the fact without any warning after years of friendship. They immediately made plans to visit that evening, and Joclyn was glad I had reached out.

When I made it to the hospital after work Joclyn had just undergone a procedure to thoroughly monitor the condition of her heart. This included the uncomfortable insertion of a scope in an artery in her thigh. She was not to move positions for at least two hours and it was very uncomfortable. She told me a cardiologist had seen her and confirmed she was experiencing major heart failure. We sat in this room waiting to be returned to her regular room and cried. We could not believe this was happening after such a great year for the both of us. Joclyn had a steady job she was enjoying, and I had begun a career in teaching that I was enjoying more than I ever could have imagined. It had been six months since our wedding and our lives were becoming exactly what we both had dreamed and planned they would become. Now our entire future came to a halt; we no longer had any idea of what was going to happen or what our lives would become. We were now just hoping for someone to tell us Joclyn was going to be alright.

Some of the doctors were optimistic. The original doctor we saw the day we checked in was confident that it was a virus that would go away. He insisted that Joclyn's heart would make a full recovery. But there were those that were much more pessimistic and felt she would be going home with an oxygen mask. The current cardiologist started preparing us for the reality that Joclyn might require a heart transplant. He even set up an appointment with a specialist in order to get her on the donor list "just in case." I had a very bad feeling that this appointment was more than a precaution. The good news was that whatever was causing the damage to her heart apparently had abated. We were told Joclyn could go home Thursday morning. This made us both happy, as this was not just Thursday, it was Thanksgiving. The news that we were going to go home also made us feel that Joclyn's heart might get better, and this could end up being just a bad week we would soon put behind us.

On Wednesday afternoon a man showed up at the door of the hospital room and announced that he was there to deliver Joclyn's "LifeVest." Joclyn and I looked at each other and we were very confused. "A LifeVest?" We both responded at the same time. "What are you talking about?" Joclyn asked. The man explained that doctors had ordered it for her to wear in case she went into cardiac arrest. I realized there was not going to be a day in this hospital that someone did not come in with some shocking news. The next thing I knew, this guy was helping Joclyn take her shirt off so he could explain how to put this large bulky uncomfortable contraption on. I lost count of how many times Joclyn asked, "Are you kidding me?" It was a lot. This really soured Joclyn's mood. Even though we were going home the next morning, this vest was going to be a reminder that our lives had taken a huge detour from normal.

The next morning was uneventful. To our relief, it looked as if we were going to get out of there as promised. I had already spoken to Joclyn's Uncle Michael who arranged an appointment with a top cardiologist in the city who was affiliated with New York–Presbyterian Hospital/Weill Cornell Medical Center. Joclyn's uncle is a doctor and we were fortunate that he was insistent that we utilize his connections to secure the best possible care for Joclyn. We were desperate to find out what had happened, and to know if her heart was going to recover. As we packed up to leave, the doctors came in with several prescriptions. Joclyn and I were anxious about the number of pills she was required to take for her heart. The one medication that we continued to find very helpful was the Lasix. Although it always led to Joclyn sprinting to the bathroom for lengthy sessions of intense urination, it also continued to help her breathing more than any of the other treatments. By 1:00 p.m., I had Joclyn back in the car and we were on the way home. It was only a few minutes by car, so we were home with the filled prescriptions by 1:30. The LifeVest was our constant reminder of our ordeal and Joclyn hated it. I was stressed about having to figure out how to clean it and put it back together correctly. Luckily, Sedaris did a good job of cheering Joclyn up with lots of kisses when we got home.

Joclyn

At some point on Monday, right as Jeremy was about to go home for the evening, a cardiologist was brought onto my case for some reason, and a decision was made to conduct an ultrasound test of my heart. The technician performing the test asked, midway through, if I have high blood pressure, and Jeremy joked that my heart looked kind of scrappy, almost like it was having a hard time. "Eh," he imitated.

Some amount of time later, enter said cardiologist. "I think you are going to be fine." He thought I was going to be fine. He may have mentioned a virus that I was sure to get over.

Another amount of time later — and this is the moment everything became horrific — enter bizarrely perky medical intern. I may make mention of this person and her words on more than one occasion. Her smile did not raise concern, but when she emoted an "Oh, my God! You have SUCH a big heart failure!" Jeremy and I could only reply with a frightened, "Whaaaat?"

The smile never left her face, seriously, even as medical professionals stampeded into my room.

It is years later, and I have yet to conjure a wittier or more appropriate reply.

I was rushed upstairs to a cardiology unit, bewildered and terrified, yet also not believing any of it. Jeremy may have, but I convinced myself that I did not have a tangible sense of foreboding, and, therefore, this lack of a sense precluded the possibility of anything bad occurring to me at that moment. I've always had a bit of a sixth sense when something was about to happen. In 8th grade, for example, I knew as soon as I walked into Spanish one day that I was going to have my surprise oral exam. I was right, even though everyone else thought it was their day and they were all wrong. They Must Be Wrong became my internal mantra. The residents (sans the insensitive lunatic who possibly intentionally vanished from my care) accompanied me to the floor, and were fairly confident that I was going to be okay. This happens, they reassured. You must have a virus that has attacked your heart. Viruses can attack anywhere. We'll get the virus under control and Then You Will Be Fine. Liking the sound of that, this I believed.

My bunkmate at this juncture became a different, skinnier older woman with a panic alarm set to ring every time she got out of bed, or, as it seemed, shifted her weight in any direction. It was needed, surely, but it was not something I needed. She also was an on the seat urinator. After telling me to relax and seeing that I was settled in, mostly, Jeremy went home. He missed the introduction into my life of yet another young doctor who has no idea of the importance of mincing one's words and speaking kindly.

"Your situation is perilous, and you will probably go home on oxygen." He was quite smug, in fact.

I reminded him that the other residents had told me that I probably had some kind of virus, and that I would be fine.

This doctor, whoever he thought he was, opened up his unthinking mouth and LAUGHED. "I wouldn't go pinning my hopes on something residents on other floors say." He really said this.

(Now I like to think of his attack as a technique for his own self-preservation since he suffered the personal burden of working at a second-rate hospital, and he put his assignment to the cardiology floor as somehow more impressive than the ones available on the general medicine floors. At least from a distance, his ID card looked like the ID cards carried by staff at the superior hospitals in the New York–Presbyterian network. Maybe he preferred Manhattan.)

He then helpfully suggested that I "get some sleep," and was sure to slap the doorway on his way out for the evening. I never knew it was possible to feel so meanly uncared for in a hospital. I almost couldn't breathe, but not because I needed more Lasix.

Jeremy had been texting me his whole walk home from the hospital, naming all of our favorite points of interest along the way.

Five Guys, Little Purity, Smiling Pizza, Gialeti's. This would become our routine throughout my multiple hospitalizations. When he would take a taxi back to Brooklyn, he would text me details about his driver, where he was, whether he was taking the bridge or the tunnel, what smelled, and all of those other things that I was unable to experience in person. When he took the subway home, he would always tell me when his F train popped out of the tunnel at Smith–9th Street. This was extra poignant because the Smith–9th notification had been a thing between us ever since we moved back to New York. Smith–9th in the afternoon signaled that he or I was two station stops away from home, and the other one would gather Sedaris for a walk and meet up at the subway station. It was wonderful. Sedaris even independently would rustle and pace when the appointed time neared, as if we'd texted her as well.

I texted Jeremy back in a panic, and he called me immediately. We both cried and lamented about how this could possibly be happening. Jeremy must have been convinced that I would not survive whatever this was, as the next day I would learn that he sent an email to Faith, my friend since childhood whom I'd not spoken to since shortly after our wedding just that past June. It seemed so trivial at the moment of heart failure, but we had fallen out with Faith and her husband Gabe over typical female wedding drama, including "It's really hard to dance to Bob Dylan" reviews. They both rushed to the hospital the next day. I didn't die though, so I guess this meant that we were friends again. At some point during my lengthy confinement, they would bring me a personalized Yankee cap and a very useful New York Times crossword book. Faith also spent several hours rubbing and hoisting my swollen hobbit feet. (Such swelling occurs during the course of heart failure, apparently.)

I vaguely recall a middle of the night, needle in the groin imaging study that very evening. I couldn't tell you what the point may have been, and later, when a similar test was performed at Weill Cornell, doctors there wondered aloud why, when this very test had been performed at Methodist, a biopsy had not been performed "since they were already in there anyway."

The Methodist Hospital cardiology team started me on a plethora of cardiac medications. I remember one called Cardizem, and I'm pretty sure I was put on oral steroids, antibiotics, and some other toxic shit. Somehow, I did begin to feel better. This circumstance made it all the crazier when a Dr. Haq gave me the name of a transplant cardiologist and told me to make an appointment to see him.

"Why on Earth would I want to meet with someone who deals with heart transplants?" I may have wondered aloud. This seemed unnecessarily impossible, and Dr. Haq backed off as soon as he recognized my reaction. "Okay, you might not need one." I rolled my eyes.

Again, this drama was completely lost on me. Later on, Jeremy would tell me that he knew, just knew that I would need a heart transplant from the first moment it was ever mentioned. So goes our luck he reasoned.

I remember wearing my Nick Swisher shirt. "You like the Yankees?" asked a different cardiologist, I think the same one from the regular medicine floor. "Yeah." They had just won the World Series, naturally, and I was wished the same good fortune as them by this doctor.

CHAPTER 5

BALLOONS AREN'T JUST FOR PARTIES

Jeremy

It is always nice to bring your wife home from the hospital. Bringing her home on Thanksgiving Day was no exception. There was still time to head out to New Jersey and join the Goldners for a full bells and whistles feast, but Joclyn was not feeling up to it. She actually felt fine with the exception of the LifeVest she now had to wear. Instead, we went home to play with the dog, and I cooked us some pasta with meat sauce. It was good to be home, but we were very stressed.

All we could think about was the appointment with the cardiologist the following Wednesday. We believed Joclyn's heart needed to show improvement so we could forget about the possibility of a heart transplant, get rid of the LifeVest, and put the whole ugly episode behind us. In our minds, a heart transplant meant the end of any kind of quality of life. We imagined a bedridden life for Joclyn. She would be loaded with bone-weakening steroids and feel exhausted all the time. I remember Joclyn commenting she might prefer death to that kind of life. The thought of all this made me sick. I was still wondering if there was any chance I could wake up and discover this was all a horrible dream. But I was really way past that point by now, and knew that I was going to have to find the strength to help Joclyn get through all of this.

The next day was encouraging. Joclyn felt even better, and I had managed to help her get her LifeVest back on after her shower.

I am usually useless with these kinds of things, but I had no choice but to figure out this contraption and become an expert on it. Joclyn had enough to deal with, I did not want to fail her and give her another thing to stress about. Later that day, Joclyn's mother dropped by and brought Thanksgiving leftovers. It was nice to eat turkey with all the fixings and enjoy, even if a day late, a normal holiday. Joclyn had a rocky relationship with her mother since she was a child, but things had improved over the past couple of years, so it was nice to have her come by and visit. We had yet to leave the house since getting back from the hospital. It was nice to have some company.

The next day was Saturday and Joclyn was still feeling fine. I thought it was time to leave the apartment and she agreed. We made plans to have dinner with Joclyn's father and his girlfriend. Do not panic: Joclyn's parents got divorced several years ago, so his girlfriend was par for the course. Joclyn and her father had a very distant relationship and rarely spoke, but when you are having "a major heart failure," as the lady at the hospital so happily blurted out, it tends to bring everyone together. Dinner was nice; being outside was even better. Heart failure? What were those doctors talking about? We could not wait to get to the cardiologist and hear him tell us that her heart was going to be fine and this was just a virus. We looked forward to him telling us we could send the LifeVest back to where it came from.

The rest of the weekend went by without incident. We became more confident everything was going to return to normal. On Monday, I was back at work. Joclyn was told she could not return to work yet, and we estimated it would be a few weeks before that changed. Monday was a breeze and before I knew it I was at work on Tuesday only a day away from taking Joclyn to one of the city's best cardiologists. It was after lunch during fifth period that I received the text from Joclyn that felt like someone punched me in the stomach. Joclyn wrote, "I feel sick. I just threw up." I immediately had a bad feeling. I hoped that it was all the medication causing the nausea. But I was worried and wanted to get home as soon as possible. The rest of the school day crawled by, and every minute seemed like an eternity. Finally the last bell rang and I was running for my car.

When I got home Joclyn was in bed and not happy. She did not have a fever, but she could not hold anything in her system without throwing up. Not even water. As the night went on her situation did not improve. We decided to get through the night and go early to her 2:00 p.m. appointment the next day. My logic was that if something happened I wanted her to be with a doctor affiliated with New York–Presbyterian/Weill Cornell Medical Center. This was a much better hospital than Methodist in Brooklyn, to which I had no plans of returning Joclyn. This was, at that time, the longest night of my life. It was much worse for Joclyn. She was throwing up constantly and could not hold anything down. Her breathing was getting worse too. I started to think she was dying. I asked her if we should go to the emergency room but she insisted it was the medication, and that we should wait till morning.

Neither of us slept much that night and we were both very scared. Morning finally came and we made one last call to the doctor from Methodist to see if this was a normal reaction to the medication. He recommended we come to the emergency room. I stood firm on my decision to avoid that hospital and loaded Joclyn into the car at 11:00 a.m. to head for the city for our 2:00 p.m. appointment. If he could not see us early, at least we were in his office just a block away from one of the city's best hospitals. While Methodist is not a bad hospital compared to most in Brooklyn, I knew moving her into the city might be a challenge once we checked in somewhere else. I wanted to make sure we got the best possible care moving forward, and I wanted the cardiologist that Joclyn's Uncle Michael had recommended. He also insisted that we would get better care at Weill Cornell.

The trip to Upper East Side was awful. Joclyn kept throwing up into a plastic container and was looking sicker by the minute. We had a travel bag packed with clothes in case we were told she needed to be admitted into the hospital. I was beginning to think that was definitely going to happen. After a few good days and some hope gathered to get past this hell, my positive attitude was diminishing rapidly. I started feeling sick myself. The thought of Joclyn being admitted into the hospital was bad enough, but not knowing what was wrong was torturous. The traffic on the FDR was no picnic either. It seemed like we had been in the car for hours when we finally got to a parking lot near the address of the office. Joclyn was pale and throwing up repeatedly. I was helpless and never felt so useless in my life. I wished I could make her better, or that I could be the one that was sick, because watching her suffer was unbearable. I practically carried her up the driveway of the parking lot and to the building next door. We got into the office and I felt a bit of relief. This was a doctor with whom we felt fortunate to get an appointment; if not for Uncle Michael's connection, we would probably have been back at Methodist in Brooklyn.

Being in the office did not help Joclyn's condition. We had more comfortable seats and now she had a bathroom to throw up in, but overall things were pretty bad. Being there so early gave me plenty of time to fill out the insurance forms while we waited. It was about 12:45 p.m. and our appointment was not for another couple of hours. I tried to keep Joclyn entertained, but as strong as she is, there are some illnesses that simply overwhelm a person's sense of humor. My jokes were not enough to take her mind off how she felt, and magazines were not doing the trick either. To Joclyn's credit, she kept her cool and remained calm. Eventually, the time had passed and we were actually asked to go in and see the Doctor at about 1:30 p.m. I guess they got tired of hearing Joclyn throw up in the bathroom out at reception. Now we got to wait in a small examination room for another 25 minutes. Of course Joclyn stopped throwing up and we joked that all her symptoms would probably go away now that we made it this far.

The doctor came into the office and we were in business. We explained what was happening. We hoped he would blame the medication for her symptoms. After an echocardiogram, the doctor took Joclyn's blood pressure. It was 60 over 40. (As my students would say, "that is MAD low.") Her heart rate was about 120. We were frightened. The doctor told us it could still be a reaction to the medication, but would be impossible to know for sure without further testing in the hospital. Then came a mutual decision between the two of us that was the difference between life and death. We were given the choice of stopping the medication and going home, followed by another visit the next day, or going to the hospital across the street for further testing. Not just any hospital, Weill Cornell had one of the most renowned cardiologists in the country. We would be in good hands. While we desperately wanted to go home and return the next day, we had both learned from past experience it was better to play it safe. We already escaped a dangerous situation when Joclyn had pneumonia a couple of years before, when a decision to avoid the hospital could have killed her.

When making the decision to go to the hospital, I also recalled a lesson I learned a few years back when I was learning to play poker. It was a "regular guy" from Maryland who had made it to the final table at the World Series of Poker that kept repeating the phrase "It is better to make a small mistake throwing away a winning hand, then making a big mistake holding on to a losing hand." If we went to the hospital even though it was not necessary, it would be a small mistake. If we chose not to go to the hospital and it cost Joclyn her life, it would be a mistake I would regret every day for the rest of my life. We made our choice. I was getting ready to put my jacket on while our doctor called ahead to cardiology and set the expectation for our arrival. Then Joclyn started throwing up again. She made it clear that even a one-block walk from the office to the hospital was not going to be possible. In a matter of minutes, we went from considering a trip home, to calling an ambulance to pick up my wife and drive her the one block to the emergency room.

The paramedics arrived about five minutes after we called. Before taking us over they took Joclyn's blood pressure and barely got a reading. One of the paramedics commented that he was amazed she was conscious. He took it again, just to be sure. He got the same result. The next thing I knew she was being loaded into the ambulance and I was given a seat at her side. A moment later we were at the emergency entrance at Weill Cornell. A team of nurses and other respondents rushed over and started hooking my wife up to all kinds of IVs, as well as a heart and blood pressure monitor. My legs started to feel weak as more and more people started to chatter and tried to explain the cause of her extremely low blood pressure and fast heart rate.

She was immediately wheeled into a private area in the back of the ER, and we were introduced to two members of the cardiology team. They appeared calm, and asked me to go through the events of the past 10–14 days leading up to this point. I felt like this was something I explained and would be explaining many times in the next few weeks. Joclyn could barely speak, and every few minutes I became less distracted by the environment around me, and got a sick feeling of helplessness as I looked down at her frightened face. All I could do was put on a brave face, and assure her that everything was going to be fine. I wished I believed those words, but any amount of comfort I could give her was worth the lie. I was not going to fool myself anymore.

I had lost hope that this was something that was going to just simply be fixed and go away. As I tried to provide support and comfort to Joclyn, I battled the fear in my head that our lives were never going to be the same. I worried that our marriage was never going to see its 7th month. I felt a despair greater than I had ever before experienced. Suddenly I was being asked all sorts of questions by a resident cardiologist. She had a friendly disposition. It was a change I welcomed. It pulled me back into the moment. As I answered her questions, Joclyn would try to chime in as well and give extra details to my responses. This added a bit of humor to one of the darkest moments of our lives. She was so stubborn and insistent on the details of her life being accurate; she actually tried contributing to the conversation while lying in a hospital bed with a blood pressure too low to measure. We knew at that moment through eye contact that if she made it through this ordeal, we would laugh about it the rest of our lives.

After some time, we were moved upstairs to the cardiology intensive care unit. While we waited, there were tests and X-rays taken. Joclyn was still up and alert. She was shocked at what was happening and shared that emotion with anybody willing to listen. Meanwhile, she was completely dehydrated. Joclyn had been unable to hold anything down for the past 36 hours, and was finally given some fluids via her IV. She was still throwing up and heaving, but nothing was coming out of her. She was moaning in pain when not trying to speak. I commented to the cardiologist on duty in this unit that I felt like she was dying, to which he replied, "she may be dying." He quickly assured me, somewhat, that they would figure out what was happening and prevent that from taking place. They were just getting in the results of the X-rays and tests, and apparently her heart was not enlarged, which was a good sign. This may have been a reaction to all the medication after all. This brought me some relief, but Joclyn was still suffering. Even with all the medication they were giving her to make her more comfortable, she was in a great deal of pain. And she kept throwing up.

The room we were in was not really a room. It was just a space. I remember how distraught Joclyn and I were when they unfolded a toilet out of the back part of the space, and showed us a curtain we could close around it. As sick as Joclyn was I could tell she was upset. We did not know how long she would be in this small space, but we had hoped she would be put in an actual room with a bathroom. This was more like an indent in the hallway. There was no place to put her stuff, and it was noisy, with lots of staff walking by all the time. This was the most critical area of the cardiology department, where people stayed when their life was in extreme danger. As unappealing as the area was, it was clear she would get the monitoring and care she needed to offer the best chance of survival. If this was not a reaction to the medication, I knew this was the beginning of a long haul. If it was the medication, and they sent us home, we still would not know if her heart was improving until the next appointment with the cardiologist.

After a couple of hours, we decided it would be best if I went home to deal with the dog. We had to pay the rent as well. It is amazing that paying the rent was on our minds, but the world around us didn't stop. Reality hit us persistently over the next few months. The plan was for me to go home and walk Sedaris, get some sleep, and take her to the kennel in Park Slope. I would then drop off the rent check and head back to the hospital. I already sent a text to my co-teachers that I would not be coming into work for the remainder of the week. Our friend Melissa would pick up Sedaris from the dog care place and bring her back to New Jersey to stay with her and her soon-to-be-fiancée, Austin. With this plan in place, I headed home. As usual, the process of leaving Joclyn in the hospital and heading home was incredibly painful. I would be riddled with guilt because I knew she always wanted me to stay longer. I reasoned with myself that I needed to sleep and get rest, but the feelings of guilt remained with me nonetheless. As I drove home, I kept wishing I would wake up so I could put this nightmare out of my memory. It was December 3rd, and I would turn 39 in a week. Dealing with a loved one with a fatal illness was not something I thought I would experience for a long time. What ended up happening was something I never anticipated I would experience at any age.

I got home and walked Sedaris. She was well aware something was wrong and not acting like herself. My usual greeting of fast and furious tail wagging and kisses was absent as she simply got up and sniffed my leg. Sedaris was Joclyn's dog before I came into the picture, and she did not like the events of the past ten days any more than we did. I climbed into bed and went to sleep. My heart was pounding and I felt terribly alone. I did not know when Joclyn would be home again, and wondered whether our lives would ever be the same. I thought about all of our plans to travel and see the world, and wondered if that was still going to be possible. I thought about our wedding day, and how happy I was that she was in my life. Later, I was told someone called me "so unlucky." But the time I already had with Joclyn made me feel like the luckiest man alive, no matter what lay ahead. Somewhere in my thoughts, I managed to fall asleep. Nothing could have prepared me for what happened next, and it is not something I would wish on my worst enemy. Joclyn and I had been married for six months of the two years we had been a couple. These were the happiest two years of my life. Suddenly everything seemed to be crashing down on us without warning.

Joclyn

On the day of discharge from Methodist Hospital, Dr. Din (from the walk-in clinic) thanked God and touched my face. I reassured him, likely too confidently, and he thanked God again. "What if I had let you go home?"

Wanting to go home and pretend that this never happened at the center of my consciousness, I paid little attention when, after the nurses told me that I no longer had to exclusively use the bathroom in my room shared with the on-the-seat urinator, I felt that walking uphill to the end of the corridor to use a more private bathroom was quite a workout. It felt like I was wearing a heavy backpack. I only realized as an afterthought that the uphill climb to the end of the hallway came with an invisible hand pushing my chest backwards, and that this was a continuing symptom of heart failure.

The horrific resident who'd told me to not "pin hopes" on anything wrote me a note for work that cited an upper respiratory infection. Seriously.

I hated the LifeVest, and loved Jeremy for operating it. When it started talking to me and mechanically announced that an irregular rhythm had been detected — it wasn't even touching me at that moment — I screamed. I didn't have to wear it while showering, and wondered just how long of a shower I could get away with. I convinced Jeremy to let me keep it off "just for one show" after bathing. "I'm still a little damp." Seriously.

It was Thanksgiving, but we didn't go to our friends' Thanksgiving dinner as planned. It was just all a little much, still. Jeremy cooked, and we nervously looked at each other and tried to be regular. My mother would bring us turkey leftovers the next evening, which normalized our lives a bit more and comforted us.

By Sunday, I really was feeling fantastic. Jeremy and I took Sedaris to the dog park in Bay Ridge — she had a best friend there, a Rhodesian Ridgeback who we joked was her Bay Ridgeback — and my biggest concern was that someone might notice the bulkiness under my jacket. My father and his girlfriend came over later that day and we walked to Johnny Mack's in Park Slope for beer and oysters. What's more non-heart failure-y than that? I wasn't short of breath and had my appetite for happy hour back.

My follow-up appointment was with a highly regarded cardiologist recommended by my Uncle Michael — why hadn't I asked for his help sooner again? — but by Tuesday afternoon I was not sure if I would hold out for medical attention until then. In the late morning I began throwing up regularly, and could not eat or drink even a thing. I took Lasix but wasn't running to the bathroom. I texted Charlene. "Uh, oh." I texted Jeremy, who panicked. I think he came home early, or at least speedily. By late that evening I had so petrified Jeremy that he called Dr. Haq, the cardiologist from Methodist who'd said "just in case." Dr. Haq said that I should come back into the Methodist E.R., but both Jeremy and I told each other it would just make more sense and that I would be seen sooner if we went to the cardiologist appointment in the morning. I think we both had just lost all trust in Methodist because of the upsetting way I had been spoken to.

I could barely tie my shoes. I wished I'd said a better goodbye to Sedaris. I dragged myself into the car. Vomiting into a Ziploc container for the entire drive was so bothering Jeremy that I wanted to be able to stop only for his sake. We parked in a lot halfway down the block from the doctor's office, and Jeremy had to push me uphill, essentially. "How could a cardiologist have steps leading into his office?" I wondered. Somehow I climbed them. Slowly, probably.

I apologized for my brazen vomiting, but the doctor acted as though this happened all the time. He jumped to no conclusions, and even suggested that perhaps it could make sense to stop all of the cardiac medications and "come back tomorrow." Like how I always ask the vet, "What would you do?" so I asked him. He admitted that he would probably not go home, and so we all decided to send me to the hospital down the street. I tried to rise, sighed, and wondered why I couldn't get up.

I was embarrassed to be carried out of a doctor's office on a stretcher. The EMTs were kind but kept looking at Jeremy and shaking their heads. Did they think I'd gone blind?

I remember lying on a gurney in the emergency room and — recurring theme — trying not to puke. When that failed, I tried to puke, which did not go over well. Jeremy was doing a lot of talking while I felt sleepy. By the time I had my own space, not quite a room but more like a glassed area, I was being fussed over and not looked at at all at the same time. I used a little sink/toilet against my will and prepared (how?) for a procedure that was described to me as "similar to an angiogram." I think this was to be the same as the middle of the night procedure I'd undergone at Methodist.

Following this procedure — "to see what is really going on in there" — I was closely monitored by Dr. Bender, one of the physicians who'd been in on my procedure. I kept falling asleep and he kept waking me up by accident as he touched and adjusted and turned the lights on and off. At some point between sleep and wake, he asked if he could call my husband. I wrote down Jeremy's number on an index card even though it was on the dry erase board on the far wall near the toilet/sink. Dr. Bender said that a balloon would help my heart. I later learned that he saved my life by staying up all night emailing Dr. Horn, his supervisor about me. "This doesn't look right."

CHAPTER 6

ZEN IS LIKE A BOTTLE OF PEPSI

Jeremy

The Doctor told me that rushing to the hospital would not really do anything to help Joclyn. I would not be allowed anywhere near her while they prepared to insert the balloon to help her artery. I could not go to sleep either. The next two hours taught me what it means to be completely alone in the world. I could not bring myself to call anyone at this hour of the night with this kind of news. I sat down at our desk in the office and stared into a blank computer screen. I wondered what could be happening. Why is this virus in her heart, and why can't they make it go away? And who gets a virus in his or her heart? I never even heard of such a thing. I thought about our wedding and how happy we were on our honeymoon. I wanted to be back in Dublin drinking a Guinness at the brewery, when everything was right in the world. Or at least in our world. But that trip was now ages ago. Joclyn running a 10K just five weeks before this moment was now ages ago. Somehow two hours went by as I sat there. I began thinking about how I needed to get Sedaris to the kennel so I could get to the hospital without worrying about her or having to come home for her. The images of my life without Joclyn were distracting me. I had to focus on a few more mundane tasks, so I could get to the hospital.

Suddenly I woke up in that chair in the office. I had fallen asleep for about ten minutes and the phone was ringing. Caller ID confirmed it was the hospital again. My hands back to a calm tremble, I picked up the phone and held my breath. The procedure was a success and the balloon was helping. It was 7:00 a.m. and my wife was still alive. But the force that was killing her was still present. How long could they keep her alive? I was happy for the news, but still desperate for some hope that she had a chance to survive this nightmare. Hope is a double-edged sword. It is a feeling of admitting you are powerless and not in control of a situation, while providing the comfort and encouragement that the situation will change for the better. To this day, I am not sure if I hate it or love it. It was getting close to the time I could drop Sedaris off and figure out where I was going to leave the rent check in a place my landlord would be able to find. It is amazing to worry about paying the rent at a time like this, but maybe I was trying to hold on to something normal and stable in my life. It was December 4th, and the rent was due. It was predictable and made sense.

I must have fallen back to sleep, or I may have passed out from all the stress. I will never be sure. Suddenly the ringing of the phone awakened me. It was the hospital again and it was about 8:45 a.m. I panicked that I had fallen asleep and missed something that would lead to the loss of my wife. I was no longer being rational. "Hullo?" After a delay of about three seconds, "Jeremy, it is Joclyn." I was so happy to hear her voice and so confused at the same time. She explained that she was going to need open-heart surgery. Then she confirmed this was definitely my wife by asking, "Can you believe that?" Only Joclyn could make a cheerfully skeptical remark like that right after she was told she needed open-heart surgery. She asked me to hurry and get to the hospital. I was already throwing on clothes and explained that I was going to drop off Sedaris and be right over. She told me she had to go but wanted to tell me herself and hung up. As I rushed Sedaris into the car I began to wonder what cutting into her chest was going to accomplish. I did not get to ask what the surgery was for, or what good would come from it. All I knew was that I had to get there. I was convinced that these were the last moments of her life and I was in Brooklyn worrying about the rent. I dropped off Sedaris and headed back to the apartment to lock up since it was on the way to the Prospect Expressway anyway.

When I got back to our apartment my landlord was mulling around outside. I ran inside and got the rent check and came out to give it to him. I must have looked like shit, because he paused when he looked at me and asked if I was all right. My landlord at the time was an eighty-year-old Italian, and it surprised me how easily he recognized I was under duress. I told him Joclyn was very sick and I needed to go to the hospital to see her. He grabbed my hand and told me that she would be okay because she is young, and pointed to his heart. I did not have it in me to tell him what was actually going on, but he knew it must have been bad because tears were pouring out of my eyes like a fountain and falling to the ground in front of us. I ran for the car and he went on his way, rent check in hand. As I got in the car I heard a familiar voice, "Jeremy!" I turned to find my neighbor Brendan with his little French bulldog Oscar in tow.

I realized that with the exception of my landlord, I had not spoken to anyone about what was going on with Joclyn. It did not take Brendon very long to figure out something was very wrong. He knew Joclyn had been sick and in the hospital, and my look and appearance suggested things were not improving. I tried to tell him what was happening, but all I could get out was "I am losing her." I broke down as I must have really needed to talk about this with somebody. I could no longer hold in the anxiety and overwhelming fear I was experiencing. Seeing a friend knocked down my wall and let everything come tumbling out. Brendan grabbed me and gave me a hug. He assured me that if she was in the hospital they would help her, and that they knew what they were doing. While I knew he was reaching for the right words, with no real understanding of what was happening, it helped to have someone else thinking about her at that moment. This simple exchange gave me the strength to get into the car and make the drive to the Upper East Side of Manhattan.

I drove like a New York City taxi driver. Literally. I was cutting people off and switching lanes, and that was in the Battery Tunnel. As I got closer to the hospital, it became more urgent that I arrive there in the next few seconds. I knew it would be another hour or two until they brought her down for the surgery, but I needed to be there with her. Sedaris was taken care of for as long as we needed. There was nothing left to pull me away from the hospital. I had a change of clothes with me, knowing that I was probably going to spend the night in the city with Gabe and Faith who lived on the Upper West Side. Their apartment was a quick and easy drive or bus ride away from the hospital. The falling out we had with Gabe and Faith was brought into perspective given the threat to Joclyn's life, and our issues were swiftly swept under the rug.

I did not know that this would be the first of many times I was anxious to get there, to be with my wife to comfort her. On this day, I thought it might be my last chance to say goodbye. My last chance to make her understand what she did for me, and how she changed my life. As I headed up the FDR, I continued fighting the thoughts of what I was going to do if she died.

I knew exactly where I was going to park the car. Although it seemed like ages ago, it had been only 24 hours since I had parked there. I did not want to look for a place that might be closer; I knew this place was a couple of blocks away and that it would be quick. I ran from the lot towards the hospital entrance a couple of blocks away. I heard my phone ringing and took a look to see who it was. I was terrified it was the hospital with more bad news. I saw that it was my brother Lee. I picked up the phone and remembered that I must have called my father the night before and told him we were back in the hospital. My father must have passed the news on to the rest of the family.

Lee was calling to find out what was going on. As I ran and tried to explain what was happening, I could feel the distress in my brother's voice. He loved Joclyn, as did his family. It was hard not to love her. She is honest and easy going, very patient, and my brother's family sensed that better than anyone. I was crying to my brother like I was ten years old again. I told him that I did not understand what open-heart surgery was going to do, and how it would stop whatever was causing this to happen. He agreed, sounding as helpless as I was; it made no sense. Lee offered to fly over from California. I told him to hold off. I wanted him to come more than anything, but if I agreed that would have made this way too real. He told me our father was packing and getting ready to head up with my other brother, Matthew, from North Carolina. This relieved me. Soon, I would have some family with me to help deal with what was happening. As I got to the entrance of the hospital, I hung up and told Lee I would call him later.

I ran through the hospital to the elevator and headed to the ninth floor. I navigated through a maze of hallways that would normally have me lost and asking directions. But not today. When I entered the room Joclyn was hooked up to countless bags of medications pumping into her arm, along with a thicker tube going into an artery in her neck. This was called a "swan" and its purpose was to monitor her heart. It made moving her neck impossible, and looked horribly uncomfortable. The one positive was that Joclyn was not throwing up anymore. She smiled when she saw me; holding back more tears, I smiled back and told her everything would be okay. In my mind I had no idea how she would be okay, but I wanted to comfort her. I still had no idea what the purpose of the surgery was and how it was going to help stop whatever it was that was causing this calamity.

Joclyn was very thirsty. She was not being given any liquids in preparation for the surgery, and she felt completely dry and dehydrated. She told me she wanted a Pepsi. I told her I would have it for her as soon as she was allowed to drink again, and joked that Manny (my father) would be beaming with pride. My father loves Pepsi, perhaps more than any man alive. Joclyn smiled and agreed. It still amazes me that we were able to think of humorous things and smile about them given the situation. Many people have since imagined that ability is common or easy to do, with no appreciation of how much strength it took for my wife and I to maintain our personalities, appreciate humor, and even just keep our sanity. I just know that it made her a hero in my eyes, as strong as anyone I had ever met. I know if I had been in her place I would have been screaming, crying, and completely inconsolable. And I have no shame admitting it. In the middle of a health crisis that was as grave as such things get, Joclyn wanted a Pepsi.

Soon after I settled into the room, someone, clearly a doctor, came into the room and introduced himself as Dr. Chen. He told us that he would be the surgeon who would perform the operation. I wondered if he was going to explain how surgery could possibly help. He must have read the expression on my face. He smiled and told me he would explain everything to me, and that my wife was going to be okay. I forgot that I was probably white as a ghost, and must have looked terrified to anyone who looked at me. He then said a word Joclyn and I will never forget, "Zen." I forget the exact context in which he used it, but he was not only showing us how to get through this crisis, he was showing us how he is able to perform such delicate surgeries where so much is at stake. I found out that Dr. Chen usually performs open-heart surgeries on children. This made me feel better, as I reasoned to myself that he had excellent hands that can work in the smallest of spaces.

Dr. Chen sat down to fill me in on what was happening and why they were going to open up my wife's chest and put her through such an extreme and dangerous operation. He informed us that Joclyn was experiencing complete heart failure. Just as he was explaining this, Dr. Horn entered the room. Dr. Horn is the person in charge of the cardiology unit at Weill Cornell and who Dr. Bender was up exchanging emails with all night, and is one of the top doctors in her field. We were suddenly surrounded by the best of the best, assuring us the best chances of success. Dr. Horn quickly explained that Joclyn had myocarditis, which was a swelling of the valves in her heart. The only thing in question was the cause of it. She explained that in almost all cases a virus causes it, but in some extremely rare cases it could be an autoimmune disease known as giant cell myocarditis.

Joclyn and I looked at each other and knew that was it. We just knew. Dr. Chen saw us do this and almost laughed. He shook his head and explained that giant cell myocarditis is an extremely rare disorder. Joclyn and I related her past bouts with autoimmune disorders. The J-pouch inside her that replaced her colon was a result of an autoimmune disorder. She has celiac disease, an autoimmune disorder preventing her from eating wheat gluten. This among a few others had us convinced it was giant cell. Dr. Chen assured us the only relationship these disorders had in common was the patient. We did not buy it. Dr. Horn wanted a sliver of the heart to perform a biopsy. Dr. Chen did not think it was likely that a small piece of the heart would reveal much, but Dr. Horn was very clear: "Get me a piece of that heart." She left the room. Dr. Chen smiled and agreed he would get her the slither of heart for her biopsy but seemed to remain very skeptical. Needless to say, my own heart was in distress as I thought carefully about the words "sliver" and "heart." Finally, I was going to find out what he was going to do, and how it would help.

He started by using an analogy of riding on a two-person bicycle with Lance Armstrong. He explained that the passenger would not have to worry about doing too much of the work making the bike move, if Lance was happy to do it himself. That made sense. I nodded my head. Joclyn was quiet, I am sure, fantasizing about the Pepsi I promised her afterwards. Dr. Chen explained that since Joclyn's heart was failing to do the work on its own, they would hook her up to a device that would do the work for her heart. This would allow her heart to relax as if it was a passenger on a dual bicycle with Lance. This would assure that blood would successfully be pumped to her organs and brain and keep her alive. This way they could deal with whatever was going on with her heart, and buy her the time needed for a heart to become available if a transplant was going to be required. Dr. Chen explained how the device worked. It was all very technical and beyond my understanding at that moment in my life. I instead asked the one question that jumped to the top of my head and needed to be answered: "What are the odds of success?"

For the past six hours, I thought hope was gone. I was going to lose my wife, and our fates were sealed. Now I had been given a viable plan, a plan that made sense and started to clear a path for life and survival. I wanted to know how viable the plan was and if it was safe to allow hope to return. Losing it the first time was so difficult, and I did not feel I could go through it again; I needed to be careful before I accepted it back into my heart. Dr. Chen smiled and told me he was 99% certain it was going to work. He looked at me and repeated, "Zen." He explained that the device being connected to her heart was a temporary one called a "CentriMag." It would connect to both the left and right ventricles in her heart, and there would be two tubes going into her heart, and two tubes going to a big machine. The machine would pump blood in and out of her body, actually functioning as her heart. This would be the solution for about two weeks until a decision had to be made for the next step. Joclyn's doctors would determine the next step after they had looked at the condition of both sides of her heart.

Since the right side of the heart does not do nearly as much work as the left, there was a chance that the longer-term solution would not involve assisting the right side of the heart. It was the left side of the heart that had the responsibility of pumping the blood to all the critical locations in Joclyn's body. If her heart recovered enough in 10–14 days, Joclyn would have an "LVAD" placed inside her body, and this "LVAD" would be an internal pump that helped the left side of the heart pump efficiently. It is a small device, and Joclyn would have to wear a battery pack. I would be trained on how to make sure it kept running and how to assure it was always charged. The thin tube and wire going into her body would have to be kept clean, but the insertion would be small and not difficult to manage. This device would remain with us until her heart both recovered and healed on its own, or until a donor heart was available for a transplant. The device was typically referred to as a bridge to a heart transplant. Dr. Chen made it obvious that she would almost definitely require a transplant. This fact escaped Joclyn, who in her exhaustion missed the doctor's implication. She made a comment that her heart could get better and she did not think she would need a transplant. It was obvious to me that Dr. Chen was just trying to avoid upsetting her when he nodded in agreement.

Dr. Chen moved on to the third option while I was quickly considering what I had just confirmed in my mind. Joclyn was going to need a heart transplant. This was going to happen. One would think I would be freaked out and traumatized by this news, but I was not. Two major things that made this news tolerable distracted me. The first was that there was hope my wife would live after all. This new hero in my life was confidently telling me how our lives would continue, and this certain death I thought was in store for my wife was no longer so certain. The second was my realization that this was going to be a major change in our lives and the next year was going to be shockingly different than I ever could have imagined just 24 hours ago. Suddenly I was going to be trained on a device that kept my wife alive while we waited for a call that would result in a ride to the hospital for a heart transplant. Dr. Chen's voice continuing with the third option pulled me out of my reverie and back to the moment at hand.

The third option was a bigger device to replace the "CentriMag" if the right side of her heart was unable to function on its own. It is a much bigger device than the LVAD and would not be unlike wheeling around a travel-sized suitcase. It also would entail a larger entry point into her body, and I would have to be trained on how to clean the wound and prevent infection. The battery life is not as long either, so Joclyn would not be going very far from home with this option. I dreaded this option. Even going home with the LVAD would be enough of a stressful responsibility; the thought of this bigger contraption that would require cleaning wounds and changing bandages was overwhelming. It would be about ten days until we knew which device would be used, if any at all. Although it was not made clear to Joclyn, the final outcome was going to be a heart transplant. The goal was to survive until there was a heart available.

Dr. Chen made it very clear that waiting for the heart was not going to be a smooth process. He warned that there would be bumps along the way. Every solution to a problem could lead to other potential problems that would need to be managed. He encouraged us to remember the word "Zen," and conveyed confidence that we would make it through this and survive. When the topic of a heart transplant came up, Joclyn and I both asked what quality of life can be expected after such a procedure? We still imagined what we both saw on the news when we were younger. Usually a heart recipient appeared sick, weak, and fragile. The life expectancy was not very long even if the operation was a success. And then, of course, we had the danger of organ rejection to consider. With so much to process, it was a wonder I was able to stand and have this conversation.

Dr. Chen smiled and told us a lot had changed in the past twenty years. He assured us both that not only would Joclyn have a high quality of life with a new heart, but that she would be running long distances again in no time. He assured us that Joclyn would be closely monitored after the transplant, and she would be taking medication to prevent her body from rejecting the new heart. Dr. Chen assured us the danger of rejection was not detecting it on time, and leaving the condition untreated. Joclyn's new heart would be carefully monitored. The post-transplant doctors would perform biopsies routinely for the rest of Joclyn's life. These biopsies will check to make sure the white blood cells created by her own immune system were not attacking her heart like a foreign invasion. This information reinforced the feeling that our lives would be forever impacted.

My phone started to buzz, and I was happy for the excuse to slide out of the small ICU room in which we were scrunched up. It was Jack Falzone, a lifelong friend and the older brother of my closest childhood friend David. In many ways Jack was like an older brother to me, and is a very close friend and always will be. I forget how he even knew what was going on; the past 24 hours were such a blur to me. I do not remember making any calls but word was out that Joclyn was gravely sick, and it was not a fact I could deny or dispel. When I told Jack she was moments away from open-heart surgery, he was silent. I could feel the utter shock in that moment of silence; just saying it out loud was shocking and I felt dizzy as soon as the words came out of my mouth. Finally, "I am sick right now, but if there is anything I can do let me know." It was nice to hear those kinds of words and that kind of sentiment. But at that moment I realized something that was very chilling. There was nothing Jack could do for Joclyn or me. There was nothing anyone could do for us. My stomach turned as this feeling of helplessness overcame me. How would anyone help us; a willing friend offered me anything I needed and I could not think of a single thing I could ask for. I only wanted one thing, and that was for Joclyn to make it through this nightmare.

The call from Jack was the first of several that were all pretty similar in context. I have no memory of calling him, but somehow in my numbness I managed to speak with Joclyn's father Marc. I do not remember the conversation, but in those moments at the hospital I do remember being aware that he was on his way. Joclyn and I had not spent a lot of time with Marc during the past two years I was with her, but he was making efforts to spend more time with us during the past few weeks when he heard Joclyn was sick. We had just dined with him and his girlfriend Cheryl a week earlier when Joclyn came home from Methodist. It seemed like an eternity had passed since that pleasant occasion. Only five days earlier we had expected positive news from our new cardiologist — that

Joclyn's was on the mend and that she could expect a full recovery. We went out to dinner to celebrate Joclyn's recovery and discharge from the hospital. Now I was waiting for Marc to arrive so I could explain why his daughter needed to have her chest cut open for a complicated operation that could end of her life.

As I fielded calls and waited for Marc, a short young woman with dark hair entered the tiny space called a room and introduced herself to us as the social worker. She reminded me of a close friend Christine, whom I had attended college with, and was also a hospital social worker. Christine moved to California several years ago. Now, I wished she were still in New York. My friendship with Christine, and my understanding of the work she did, made it easier to like this social worker, who was there to ensure Joclyn was an adequate recipient of a donor heart. She asked me a number of deeply personal questions that probably would have offended me in different circumstances. I understood she was doing her job, and remembered how Christine explained the more cooperative you are to social workers, the more they will go out of their way to help you. Just like in all areas of life, you get out what you put in, and this lady was, after all, just doing her job. I smiled and was patient as she asked questions you would never expect from a stranger you met five minutes earlier. I calmly answered these personal questions, which went way beyond personal finances. My effort was appreciated and rewarded with smiles and offers of any assistance she could provide.

Before one receives a donor heart, which is not easy to acquire, one must show that one's lifestyle is suitable and that the heart will not be wasted. As I was explaining that we will not end up homeless and have the funds put away to ensure our rent, I started to feel relieved that I put away money my whole life in case of a scenario just like this one. I have always tried to live a very sensible life when it came to finances. While Joclyn and I both enjoyed the simple pleasures in life, we were careful with our money, and always made careful financial decisions. I was proud that I could confidently say I was able to financially support my wife and assure the appropriate accommodations she would need in her rehabilitation.

Speaking with the social worker about how we would live in our new scenario made me realize there was an important issue I needed to discuss with Joclyn. If anything happened to her, I was completely unprepared and lacking some important information. I did not have passwords to certain accounts, and had no idea how I would deal with certain details regarding her estate. It is a horrible thing to have cross your mind, but the reality was I would have been lost on some of these things if something had gone wrong in surgery. I was as gentle as possible as I asked her for certain passwords and the locations of important paperwork. I reminded her it was information we should have already shared, that my asking was just a precaution, and that I believed she was going to make it through all of this because she is a fighter.

As the reality of the situation crept back in I felt two hands squeeze my shoulders. Joclyn's father was there, and it was a big relief. I was not alone anymore, I had someone there to share this maddening situation with who was as upset and afraid as I was. I felt a lot of weight leave my shoulders and I noted that Joclyn was happy to see her father there as well.

I am not really sure why Joclyn and her father are not closer, or how it was possible I had only met him a few times when we all lived in the same borough. Joclyn's mother, who had her own issues to manage, had made life quite difficult for Joclyn and her father, and this had strained their relationship. But since the divorce, Joclyn hoped things would have gotten better. Still, when Joclyn and her father planned get-togethers, they were often postponed. Short text messages replaced phone calls as their primary means of communication. I visited this topic with Marc in the weeks to follow. He shared that he carries a lot of guilt about his past relationship with Joclyn. However, I still haven't figured out exactly why their relationship still remained so strained.

The social worker finished with the questions and assured me we had no red flags, and that Joclyn was a good candidate for a donor heart. I got up and took a few more calls from random family members and friends. My father called and told me he was almost packed and would be leaving for New York the next day. Faith called and said she would get to the hospital that evening, and insisted I stay with her and Gabe that night. I greatly appreciated her invitation. I would wake up just a short and easy crosstown bus ride from Joclyn's hospital room.

Several doctors arrived in Joclyn's room and introduced themselves. Each described his or her role in Joclyn's upcoming operation. We were getting close and the stress was growing inside of me; I actually felt Marc help me back up to a standing position. Joclyn was nervous but anxious to get it over with, desperate for the relief from total nausea and complete dehydration. She kept reminding me to have that Pepsi for her when she woke up. I reminded her that Pepsi was an easy item to find in New York City. She looked me straight in the eye and said, "and don't try to bring me that Pepsi Free shit or diet crap. I want the sugar and the caffeine." I promised her pure "Grade A" Pepsi and she smiled. Time was drawing closer and I tried to fight the thoughts that this could be the last conversation I had with my wife. She was in grave danger; this was an emergency open-heart surgery, and she was not in ideal condition for it. Even the heart transplant itself would not be nearly as life-threatening, as that would occur when she was in better condition. This was real. I could lose her on this day. I would have lost her yesterday if our cardiologist appointment had been a day later.

While all these concerns ran through my mind, Joclyn worried only about one thing: more than a fear of death, all Joclyn could talk about was not wanting to wake up on the operating table. I assured her this would not — and all but certainly could not — happen. But for some reason she was convinced it could happen. I told her it would not happen, and even if it did, they would put her back under and she would have no memory of it happening. All this accomplished was to fuel her suspicion that it could happen. I promised her it would not happen, and had every nurse and doctor that came into the room assure her it would not happen. Joclyn said something about being the type of person that could wake up under anesthesia, which would normally have had me rolling on the floor. But I was too worried for her life to see the humor in the situation, and was desperately trying to get her in a better frame of mind before the surgery. She did calm down eventually, and I thought she just needed to focus on something else other than the possibility of never waking up again.

As they wheeled her out of the room I followed her all the way to the elevator. At this point Marc had to stay put, but I got to ride down with my wife. When we got out of the elevator the staff told me I could not go any farther. I told Joclyn that I loved her and would see her soon. She told me she loved me and to remember the Pepsi. I cried as the elevator doors closed and took me back up to meet Marc. I wished it was I who was sick, and that Joclyn was the one in robust health. I felt helpless, but at least her life was in the hands of some of the best surgeons in the country. But they were still strangers. When I got back to Marc he looked as distraught as I felt. We decided that four to five hours in a waiting room was not going to work for us. We headed for the Irish pub down the street. I knew it was there because it was near the parking lot where I left the car. I wondered how I could eat at a time like this as I stared down at the menu. It occurred to me that I had not eaten in over 24 hours. I am not a very good Jew so 24 hours of fasting was not chartered territory, and certainly a personal record. We both ordered a beer and some food. Considering all that stress, those chicken tenders were really tasty.

Dr. Chen had my cell phone number so I brushed off any guilty feelings about leaving with the rationale that finding nourishment would have no impact on the results of the operation. If something happened, sitting in a depressing waiting room was not going to make a difference. I also wanted time to pass more quickly. Marc felt the same way, and admitted he needed at least one drink. We were trying to relax and take our minds off what was happening to our girl. We must have been there for two hours, and I must have fielded over twenty phone calls. The word was out and everyone wanted to help and offer their support. I profoundly appreciated every offer, but each was a painful reminder that only the passage of time would help at this point. I had no idea what was going to happen tonight, or over the next few months. I worried that something could go wrong, that I might lose Joclyn. Suddenly I felt sick. After eating only two of the deep-fried chicken strips, I was done. I could not eat another bite. I needed to go back to the hospital.

We got to the waiting room, and I was instantly glad to be there. But I was also happy we went to the pub. I do not think I would have survived the first two hours in that stuffy, depressing room. One of the many "Are you the father" talk shows was on the television, and people were watching it as intensely as if it was the final episode of M*A*S*H. It felt like only a few minutes and my heart skipped a beat as I felt the presence of Dr. Chen before I even saw him come over to me. My initial reaction was that something was wrong because the operation was supposed to take four to five hours, not two. I was not aware that it had been four hours, and in my numbness, two more hours had passed. Dr. Chen caught my eye and smiled immediately; for this reason alone, I love the man. A smile is one of the most thoughtful and kind acts a surgeon can offer when approaching a family member after a life-threatening operation. I immediately knew that Joclyn survived, and a million pounds of weight left my shoulders. The unknown force squeezing my stomach released its grip. I was breathing freely again.

"Joclyn did great. She is a strong young lady," were the first words out of his mouth. I immediately felt a twinge of pride because I knew my wife was a fighter. She was as stubborn about not succumbing to heart disease as she was about ordering a favorite item on the menu in one of our preferred restaurants. She was determined to survive, and this regenerated me instantly and gave me a newfound confidence that she was going to overcome this and win her life back. I knew I had to stay strong and encourage her no matter how bad things became. If it was true that a positive and optimistic attitude would help her chances of survival, I was going to be the model of positivity. Up to this day, my friends remind me of how positive and sure of everything I was, while they would leave the hospital sick over the depleted condition of my wife. Most of those friends thought I was just deluding myself. The truth is, I was terrified inside. I was anything but confident. But if fifteen years of improvisation workshops taught me anything, it was how to commit to a character. If a positive character was going to increase her chances of survival, that is what Joclyn would get.

Dr. Chen told me the operation was a great success and Joclyn had done great. As soon as they attached the CentriMag, her organs came back to life. Her kidneys were back to full functionality, which relieved my concern that there was permanent damage. Most of all her heart had Lance Armstrong helping it out. Blood was pumping throughout her body. As long as that was the case she would remain alive. Dr. Chen also confirmed that her heart was beyond repair. Joclyn would need a heart transplant. I already knew that was coming, but it still stung just the same. I would have to tell her and hope she would not be too upset and discouraged. But for now, Marc and I were relieved. Joclyn had endured the first and probably most dangerous of her heart surgeries. A nurse approached us a few moments later and told us we could see Joclyn in a couple of hours after the clinical staff cleaned her up and returned her to a real room. As much as Marc wanted to stay, he told me he needed to go home but promised to return the next day.

As I waited for the okay to see Joclyn, Gabe and Faith showed up at the hospital. They came over to me with shocked faces, which helped me to realize how all this must have appeared to the outside world. As I had the whole story and was living the story, they were just getting my quick texts comprised of messages like "Joclyn going into open-heart surgery in one hour." They were relieved when I told them she was okay and out of surgery. It was not long after that a nurse came in to tell me I could go see my wife. The three of us followed her to the room. We were told we could go to the door but could not go into the recovery room. When we got to the door I looked in and saw Joclyn. She still had the breathing tube in and was awake. She saw me and reached her hand out and tried to get up. It broke my heart. She was confused and scared. I wanted to go hold her and tell her everything was okay. They held her down and told us we had to go back to the waiting room and we would not be able to see her until morning. I felt sick. Gabe looked sick. And Faith looked strong.

We decided there was no point spending the night in the waiting room since they lived a few minutes away. We headed for the exit. Gabe had a Board of Education parking permit I could use in my window, so parking would not be an issue. I would be able to leave my car outside their building without the worry of alternate side parking rules. They lived across the street from two schools and the area was all permit parking. Not long after leaving the hospital, we stopped to get some snacks, then parked and secured the cars. I knew I was a simple bus ride away from going back the next morning, but the sight of Joclyn, confused and confined in a hospital bed, haunted me. I wanted to hold her and reassure her, but felt better when Faith reminded me she would not remember a thing. I barely touched the snacks I bought. Gabe and I watched some basketball. I thought about the past 24 hours and all that had happened, then fell asleep.

I woke up early the next morning anxious to get to the hospital. I was happy my phone did not ring in the middle of the night. This provided me confidence that no issues followed the surgery. The staff in the intensive care unit assured me a nurse would constantly monitor her condition overnight. I just wanted to get there and see her as soon as I could. I hoped the breathing tube was taken out, but had no way to be sure. Some nurses warned me that some patients needed it to remain in their lungs for several days following such a major surgery. I showered and headed out for the M79 bus on 81st street as Gabe and Faith instructed me. It was a quick bus ride through the park and crosstown to York Avenue. Then I had to walk from 79th street to 67th to get to the main entrance of the hospital. The walk took an eternity and I actually started to jog. I listened to my voicemail and had confirmation that my father and brother were in the car driving north on I-95. Help was on the way.

Joclyn

Before 7 a.m., I met Dr. Chen. He came in and explained — out of what felt like nowhere — that I needed to have open-heart surgery, immediately, in order to save my life. He had already cleared his entire schedule except for a baby, and he was only going to give me that much time because he wanted to allow time for Jeremy to arrive at the hospital.

I remember pointing to myself, "Me?"

"Yes," nodded Dr. Chen.

"But they put a balloon in."

"It's not enough," he said with a dismissive wave.

I would later touch my chest, sadly, knowing it would never be the same, no matter what happened after this. A good childhood friend had had several open-heart surgeries. She was supposed to be the one among the two of us with a big scar on her chest. I already had my own scar from when my large intestine was removed nine years earlier (see "ridiculous medical history" above).

I called my aunt and radiologist uncle. "What?? Here, talk to Michael." My uncle came on the phone and basically assured me that if this is what I was told needed to be done, then this was what we would do. I wasn't in shock; I wasn't numb; I just did not understand how this could even be real or possible. I'm 32. I just ran a 10K. I eat well. I am not overweight; in fact, I'm in really good shape. I'm nice to people. I love animals. Jeremy and I have only been married for five months. The rabbi had wished for us that our wedding day would be the saddest day of our lives. How can this be fucking possible? It can't, was all I could think. I was absolutely fucking terrified.

The purpose of the surgery was to put in some pumps — specifically a "CentriMag Extracorporeal Blood Pumping System" that would do the job of my heart and would supply blood to all of my organs, some of which had apparently started to fail — which would explain why for the past two days when I took Lasix, a diuretic prescribed by the bizarrely chipper team at Methodist, I did not pee — and allow my heart to "rest" and hopefully heal from whatever had damaged it. Dr. Chen made some kind of Lance Armstrong analogy to Jeremy when he arrived. I don't know if that helped me at the time, but it seemed to make Jeremy feel better about what the outcome might be at least in terms of how he was able to hold himself together and translate the goings-on to me. Dr. Chen told Jeremy to imagine my heart as a novice cyclist, and that Lance Armstrong was to take over. My heart was to assume the role of ineffective biker, and the surgically implanted pumps would be the seven-time Tour de France contestant, and who cares if he juiced? If only it were that clean.

I learned that I had some type of myocarditis, as had been theorized but poorly explained by the amateur team at Methodist Hospital as an inflammation of the heart. This is generally caused by a virus, I was told, and sometimes the heart can heal. If it does not heal, I would possibly need a heart transplant. As just the sound of those two words together is science fiction, I knew that this could

not be possible. No. Fucking. Way. Almost in passing, Dr. Horn —
the best of the best, I was assured (in all likelihood Bill Clinton's
cardiologist, although HIPAA privacy rules precluded this scrap of
trivia) — explained that she would also check another possibility:
that my myocarditis was caused by an "incredibly rare"
autoimmune condition. In fact, this form of myocarditis was so
"incredibly rare," and the likelihood that I suffered from it so
remote, that her insistence to "get a piece of that heart" for biopsy
was treated as an annoyance and an inconvenience — an extra
procedure for the sake of thoroughness, an extra billing code to
tack on to the inevitable debt caused by this growing catastrophe,
but with a dubious possibility of usefulness in my diagnosis. Dr.
Chen and the others in the room wanted efficiency during this
devastating time. I don't remember if Jeremy and I looked at each
other following Dr. Horn's remark, but I know that we were both
thinking at that moment that that was probably the answer. I have
seemingly a million other autoimmune disorders, so why not,
really?

A bit of background: I was diagnosed with ulcerative colitis
when I was 21, and had my entire colon removed when I was 22. I
had an ileostomy complete with ileostomy bag for two months, was
"reconnected" with a procedure known as ileoanal anastomosis or
"J-pouch," and soon after that had bilateral cataract surgery to
remove cataracts I'd developed from being on high doses of
prednisone during the effort to stave off the need for such a major
operation to control the colitis in the first place. A year following
the cataract surgery, my hair began falling out in clumps until I had
almost none left and looked cancerous; my friend Charlene came
over and shaved the rest to The Three Tenors and shots of El
Jimador, and I then learned that this was an autoimmune condition
known as alopecia areata. After visits to two dermatologists, who
did things like rub steroid cream on my head and inject my scalp
with corticosteroids, (if I hadn't seen the bottles myself, I would
have sworn in an affidavit that the product used was actually a
snake oil derivative). I went to my gastroenterologist, who
diagnosed celiac disease. My treatment for celiac disease required
that I eliminate gluten from my diet. The cause? Autoimmunity, of
course. Once I'd eliminated gluten from my diet and saw that my

hair had begun to grow back just two weeks later, I'd somewhat convinced myself that maybe I was done in the development of new yet significant medical conditions.

I don't remember when, but shortly thereafter, (time loses its linearity in the ICU) I learned that I did, in fact, have giant cell myocarditis. "Incredibly rare," they say. Go ahead. Google it. You'll learn that only 63 other people have had it, and that in all but one person, the result was either death or a heart transplant. Seriously. It was at that point that I was told that I would most definitely need a heart transplant. I guess that was better news than certain death, but I didn't really want any of this, to be honest. This is not what my life is supposed to be. I don't do anything wrong. I don't deserve this. This is beyond reasoning. All I could think about at that moment was doubt and absurdity.

These thoughts were not really helpful or productive, so I cannot really dwell in them. I want to, and my visitors expect me to, my cousin James even once saying that he would be "a whole hell of a lot angrier than [me]." What for, I wonder? People might not want to be around me if I'm like that. That would be horrible. This plus loneliness? Surviving on life support, immobile, with no visitors? Unfathomable. From end to end, I will spend nine weeks in the hospital. Jeremy came every single day even though he was working as a first-year teacher and was in graduate school two evenings a week for his second master's degree in special education. For that, I am so incredibly lucky and appreciative. At the same time, though, I can't help but also feel like that exceptional treatment is what I deserved at the very least, considering that I was given this horrendous diagnosis that no one ever heard of, and that had been hours from killing me. I deserve for the universe to eternally roll out in my favor, lottery tickets included.

CHAPTER 7

ARE THESE TUBES RED?

Jeremy

As I entered the room I saw Joclyn was sleeping. My heart stopped as I caught a glimpse of the four thick tubes coming out of her body. I expected the smaller drainage tubes, which were what you might see in any medical drama on television or in a movie. But the thick tubes, which the blood that flowed through them made red, shocked me. These tubes led to a giant machine with a bunch of numbers flicking on the display screen. I had no idea what they meant, but it seemed to be working. The rest of the room was a big step up from where we were the day before. The room was bigger, with chairs and a giant window with a great view outside, and more importantly a long ledge which acted as a countertop. This ledge would eventually be stocked with gluten-free snacks and beverages that would get Joclyn through the day. I put my jacket down and turned toward my wife as she opened her eyes and gave me a small and forced smile.

"I feel like I just got hit by a bus," were the first words she said to me after I asked the seemingly moronic "How are you feeling?" I gave a small nervous laugh, but was relieved she was speaking and apparently doing much better than the day before. "Do you have the Pepsi?" she asked me, with no care that it was 8:00 a.m. I lifted the bag and pulled out a bottle of Pepsi that I picked up on the way. I inserted the straw and Joclyn took a long deep sip and let out a long "uuuuummmmm." I was amazed that she was still craving it and did not waste any time getting to it regardless of the hour.

She thanked me for bringing the Pepsi and told me she loved me. I told her how proud I was of her, and how much stronger than me she was. She motioned to the big red tubes, and said "Did you see these? Are you fucking kidding me?" I laughed as I realized that even in the most extreme conditions, Joclyn was still Joclyn. I think the anesthesia was still in her system because the pain was not at its height yet, and we had a fairly good time in those hours of the day. The most comforting thing was the fact she was alive with functioning organs. This was evident by the urinary bag that was filled with her urine and constantly being emptied and filled again, something I would tease her about for the next nine weeks.

Joclyn

So I awoke following my first open-heart surgery to "good news!" My failing organs were no longer failing, and as soon as the pumps had been attached in the operating room, my catheter bag began filling with urine. Good news is relative to the situation, but I did not want any of this. How could my kidneys have possibly been starting to fail? The other news was that my blood was being circulated external to my body, and was visible to all who came into my room. "Are those red tubes?" my first gynecologist and obstetrician who had delivered me (who would come to visit on hearing of my predicament) would ask. "No. Clear." "Oh." Fantastic. Maybe he was weirded out because he thought he'd somehow erred during delivery. I hear those guys pay a million easy just for malpractice insurance. Thirty-two years later probably cleared him, I would imagine.

That first surgery implanted two CentriMags in my body. From here, the doctors planned another surgery two weeks down the road. In that procedure, my doctors would remove these CentriMags, and replace them with a left ventricular assistive device (LVAD). An LVAD is a smaller device that would theoretically allow me to go home while waiting for a donor heart to become available. That sentence sounds incredible. I can't have been awaiting availability of a donor heart. And if this was so safe, why did Jeremy and I both think it a good idea that I give him the passwords to my online banking accounts and instructions on which bills were paid on which websites? I didn't blink at the time, but I may have held my breath for an extra beat or two. I'm only 32 and I just got married and I recently ran a 10K and I already had my "You Must Learn that Life is Short and Precious" lessons when I was 21 and 22 and 23 and 24.

CHAPTER 8

MORPHINE AND BEDPANS

Jeremy

As I sat there and told Joclyn about all the well-wishers that were calling and sending texts, I noticed her holding a little device and clicking on this button. I asked her what it was, and she explained that it was the device that controlled the morphine drip and distributed the painkiller into her system. It is kind of ironic they would empower her with this as she was clicking it constantly without a break. Joclyn explained that eventually she would be able to go longer without clicking it. I realized why she was not screaming in pain, and why she was able to have a conversation with me. She was dosing herself aggressively with morphine. All I could think to say was "Can I have some?" Unfortunately there was a strict policy forbidding the sharing of morphine with family. Dr. Chen came into the room with his usual warm smile and checked on Joclyn. He was satisfied with the first 12 hours of recovery and reported that things could not have gone better. I gave him a look that let him know I had not told her that a heart transplant was indeed needed. I did not know how Joclyn was going to take this news. She resisted this news when I brought the subject up the day before. She insisted that her heart would be fine.

I think we silently agreed to hold off on sharing the news of a transplant with Joclyn. She was in a lot of pain despite the morphine and had been through so much in the past 36 hours. She deserved a break. Dr. Chen confirmed that the operation was a success and they would be monitoring the condition of her heart over the next ten days to determine what came next. I was hoping for the smaller device, the LVAD. I was confident I could handle that device and it would allow us to leave the house and go to restaurants and sit in the park. The "dual" device scared me. Again, it was a bigger device and would involve me cleaning a big wound and being responsible for preventing infection. I also imagined and dreaded the restrictions on mobility that life with one of these devices would surely entail. This would drive Joclyn crazy if it stretched out over a year. We had to hope that the right side of her heart improved so we could proceed with the LVAD option. We had ten days to worry about it.

After Dr. Chen left us with a high feeling of "Zen," we met Neshama, who was to become a constant figure in the rest of our ordeal.

Joclyn

Have you ever used a bedpan? Previously, I never even would have touched a bedpan, even if it were sitting on a shelf, unused, still in its original packaging, covered in dust, even at CVS.

The expectations surrounding such a toileting apparatus, which oddly resembles the pink basin from the bathing scenarios I'm sure I'll get to, are unreasonable. First, I am oddly accustomed to using the toilet while in an upright position, and this posed quite an inconvenience for the nursing staff.

Let me back up for a second and explain why I could not use an actual toilet that was attached to plumbing. Because I needed two people to help me out of bed, the whole process of moving and getting up posed an inconvenience to the nursing staff. Also, the machinery to which I was attached required a constant power source and was usually plugged into a wall outlet. For my several-times-a-week (not until later on) walking down the hall excursions, the power was switched to battery, the transition to which was also a two-person, relatively complex process. Once on battery power, I still was not able to move about independently. The CentriMag machine needed at least one person to push it along beside me.

Later, the LVAD to which I would find myself tethered would need somehow to attach to my person. I was so weak, and there were so many wires, that even shifting from the bed to a bedside commode was arguably inconvenient, as it was, almost daily, by the night staff.

So back to the first point. The typical, scripted position with which to utilize a bedpan for elimination is in BED, as in supine, as in like you are going to sleep, except that not only are you not going to sleep, you are presumably urinating or having a bowel movement, all while horizontal and very much awake. Since 2001, I have not been privy to the feeling of possessing a large intestine; since 2000, I have I not known the experience of a dutiful large intestine. But I do seem to recall receiving the most comfort from going to the bathroom when it was done upright and while surrounded by porcelain and privacy. I do suspect that my unique intestinal setup added to the discomfort and peculiarity of attempting to relieve myself in this degrading way, but still. How much better could it be for someone else?

Despite my extensive gastrointestinal history, I only soiled myself once while hospitalized. It was totally unrelated to my daily bedpan refusal fiasco, shockingly. It had instead to do with a bizarrely unexpected drug interaction. I don't remember why, but I was given intravenous lidocaine. Actually, I'm not sure if this is what did it, but it occurred within seconds of the drug being "pushed" into my IV line, so it seems pretty likely that it was the culprit. All of a sudden, with one of my favorite nurses who always talked about her new puppy in the room, I heard a very strange noise in my ears, a *"woo-woo-woo,"* if you will. I felt tingly and felt like I was both about to pee on myself and possibly have an orgasm, but not in a good way. I saw black spots and thought I might pass out. My mouth became very dry. I tried to explain what was happening, and help was summoned in the form of another cute nurse with funny stories. I heard my favorite nurse yell, "Help!" I don't recall the remedy; some type of lidocaine reversal antidote was injected, possibly, and I felt better pretty quickly. When I returned to normal (relative,) I realized that the sheet under me was damp, and my one pair of hospital pants that my friend Jena the occupational therapist (with whom I'd gone to occupational therapy school) had brought me from the maternity unit had a big, ole shit stain in them. Goddammit. What even happened there? God knows I've had tons of lidocaine since, albeit not intravenous. My doctors regularly inject the drug into the side of my neck in preparation for my frequent right heart biopsies and cardiac catheterizations; I suffer no adverse consequences from these doses of lidocaine, so go figure.

On an outpatient basis, as it turns out, Lidocaine is a great condiment. It burns brutally going in, but it allows then for the insertion of a catheter which I've yet to ever look at, lest I remember how thick it is and picture it and tense up and make the whole process somehow more difficult. Lying in a pseudo-operating room while attached to a constantly inflating and deflating blood pressure cuff and hearing phrases like "I'm now collecting four little pieces of your heart for biopsy," and then actually hearing snipping noises, feeling fluttering in my chest, and the occasional sharp pain (as some of my plentiful scar tissue is nicked by the knife that is attached to the end of the catheter) is difficult enough. Some doctors will say things like "too much Lidocaine will collapse the vein and then we won't be able to do this," but others understand that if I'm in agony, I won't be able to do this. The understanding doctors lay it on thick. I really like them.

When the reluctant staff forced me to use a bedpan, I insisted that the bed be elevated into "the chair position," which involved, well, just what it sounds like. The back of the bed would be raised all the way up to a vertical position so the bed resembled a giant throne for an invalid king or queen. Just nuts. Nuts. What made this even more traumatic was that it was just for defecating. I didn't ever urinate because I was attached to a Foley catheter, adding the bonus of a steamy bag of urine attached to my body as an accouterment needing to be moved as I went to the restroom.

I mean, I was attached to a Foley catheter until, one day, when every time I moved, urine poured out of me, completely bypassing the Foley. Neshama, the nurse in charge of the LVAD, dubbed "Dr. Gloom-and-Doom" by my father and Jeremy, took the opportunity to insist that I allow the catheter to be removed and only use the bedpan or commode to urinate.

I could not understand how they could not understand why I feared this planned catheter removal. Generally, people urinate more often than they defecate. This even applies to me — sans large intestine. Was I really now to be expected to use the bathroom even more often? Oh, and I was still taking Lasix a few times a day, which induces frequent urination, on top of my already inconvenient but nonetheless normal frequency of urination.

CHAPTER 9

DEFINITELY ISRAELI

Jeremy

Neshama was not really a doctor; I have since learned that she is a nurse practitioner. But at that time, we assumed everyone in a white coat was a doctor. She introduced herself as a specialist on the CentriMag machines that functioned as Joclyn's heart, and explained she would be training me on becoming LVAD certified. She warned me that I would be tested in a way that suggested I might not be able to pass. She told me this was serious business and that I had better study. Marc was in the room while this was taking place and also wanted to learn this information as well. Neshama turned to him, and it was clear he impressed her no more than I did.

Neshama told us that she would be back to teach us how to put on sterile gloves without infecting them. As she left the room Joclyn looked at me and said, "Israeli, definitely." Laughing at Joclyn's comment, I immediately visualized Neshama holding a machine gun to my head and shouting, "Clean the wound! Clean it!" Neshama would in fact show us that kind of resolve and toughness in the course of protecting Joclyn's health. But I'll explain that later.

Joclyn

Neshama really was the bone in the bite of fish — sometimes. She tempered every measure of good news she delivered with her vision that events could, and probably would, take a turn for the worse.

When being discharged home with an LVAD was a possibility we discussed, although Jeremy and I realized that there were significant burdens to bear, we were excited. Going home still was going home, even if it meant that Jeremy had to perfect sterile technique for glove donning and wound dressing. Neshama almost made it sound as though perhaps we would all be better off if I spent the rest of my life in the hospital. She presented us with a lecture on all of the otherwise seemingly harmless activities in which an LVAD patient was not to engage, lest sudden death occur. "Even a non-serious car accident, the seat belt, or even just a regular shower, you're dead!" Well, that might not be the best example, but she was the rain on the parade before the parade-goers had even assembled.

CHAPTER 10

CAN WE GET A HUMIDIFIER IN HERE?

OR A HAIRDRESSER?

Jeremy

Nurses would come into the room, and Marc and I had to leave while they did some cleanup routine. This would happen over the next five to six weeks. Everyone was ordered out of the room for a cleaning ritual that would usually last about 30 minutes. Joclyn was upset because she was too weak and constricted to use a cell phone at this point. She worried that I would not know when to return to the room. I promised her I would keep checking and would not be gone too long. Marc and I headed to the cafeteria to grab some food. Then we hung out in this waiting room that had a couple of TVs, some tables, and a few couches. I called my father and he and my brother were just south of D.C. heading up I-95. He was driving towards his longtime friends Hal and Winnie's house in New Jersey. My father and brother would stop there and spend the night, and arrive at the hospital in the morning. I realized it was Friday. I could not believe how much had changed in a week. Normally, I would be at work at this time thinking about where we would go for dinner that night. The nurse came in and told us we could return to Joclyn. When we got back to the room, Joclyn's mother was there.

Leslie was taking fairly well the sight of her daughter and the tubes entering and exiting her body. She appeared calm and was in good spirits. I wondered if this was strength or just denial. Her husband Jay, whom she had recently married, was somewhere parking the car. A month before this all happened, nobody in the room would have planned for this get-together. Joclyn's parents had been divorced for several years and I do not think they were each other's preferred company. I did see them together when I met Marc for the first time. We were at Joclyn's sister Rachel's camp on visiting day. The camp actually held the Bat Mitzvah and Bar Mitzvah of all the kids of age who chose to have it there. Rachel shared her day along with a couple of other girls, and Joclyn thought this would be the perfect time for me to meet her sister. Now, here we were with both parents in one room under a completely new circumstance. Marc did not stay long. After kissing Joclyn goodbye, he told me he would return the next day, and left. It was about 5:00 p.m. when I had confirmation my father had made it to New Jersey and would arrive the next morning. After a few hours, Leslie left and Joclyn and I finally spoke about everything that had happened. We were both still shocked.

Joclyn

Brushing my teeth had never seemed so important before it became one of the few things I could do for myself. Actually, due to my limited mobility, I could not gather the supplies needed or assume an appropriate position for the task. That someone would not bring me dental hygiene products unless I asked made me a very proactive asker. It seemed outrageous that a doctor might expect to speak with me, or a technician could X-ray my chest, portably, without allowing me to first clean my teeth. Jeremy had brought me my own fancy battery powered toothbrush, and Faith had purchased a stand-up tube of Tom's of Maine high-end toothpaste. Due to the high concentration of supplies I'd amassed, the resultant difficulty for nurses in a hurry to locate particular versions of a requested item, and my endless willingness to not be a bother, they remained largely unused. I ended up about half the time with the subpar hospital issue toothbrush, the kind that comes in an individual straw-like wrapper, and whose bristles came out in my mouth. The hospital-grade toothpaste may have been Made in

China, and was more fakey than minty, and the mouthwash contained no alcohol, thus was not terribly effective, but did possibly satisfy some sort of contraband requirement for the psychiatric floor's dual diagnosis program.

My skin was always dry. Left untreated, my skin would always be dry under non-hospitalized circumstances anyway (except for my nose!), but hospital air went out of its way to make me finally understand what dark-skinned people mean when they complain of being "ashy." I must have gone through ten tubes of hand lotion of various economic classes. When our friends John and Maria Lennon drove up from Philadelphia one night, and Maria insisted that I keep the large, pump style bottle of Eucerin she kept in her purse, I was so excited I could have devoured its contents.

Happy hand lotion application dominates the memory of my aunt and uncle's visit balanced by the frustration I felt at following at least five minutes behind their conversation. I cannot write as quickly as the rest of the world speaks. Why, yes, I did lose my voice at some point from being intubated and extubated so many times Doesn't everyone?

I wondered how much luckier other hospitalized people were than I.

While waiting for a heart, the bathing process was a neat and safe little package. I kind of enjoyed it. The care was so thorough and so personal and made me feel so dependent and ridiculous, but I think I might have thought or believed that I would be okay, and that a heart would come and I would get to go home and live my life and be fine because they took so much time to ensure my comfort in the cardiac ICU — and cleanliness — that it couldn't possibly be for naught. It was to preserve me for After. So I Could Continue.

Bathing ended the day at Weill Cornell, so it was always postponed until after Jeremy left for the evening. I was pretty much supine for a lot of the time, and so the bathing took place in bed. It was an enormous, two- or three-person ordeal for me to transfer in and out of bed or a chair or a toilet, so bathing also ended my sitting for the day. I always pushed for the process to occur as late as possible so it would also coincide with medication delivery, including the life-saving Zyprexa (the drug that made me sleep and stop seeing yellow things on the walls). I wonder if this preference was for the routine of things. I craved some kind of attachment to the way life is supposed to be lived, as opposed to laying awake all night in a critical care unit, the occasional moan horrifying me. Most of the nurses were younger than I and, while so compassionate and wonderful, I so doubted could imagine themselves in my shoes — or gown, as it were.

The nurses were so kind, and they were Arvin and Derrick, and women — I can never remember women's names. The first thing they would do is prepare the pink basin. As a hospital-based occupational therapist, I am very familiar with the pink basin from working on self-care skills with clients. I was never this familiar. They would fill it with warm water and would sometimes add the liquid soap that Jeremy brought from home, probably to add a touch of customary sanity to this process. They would combine this liquid with purpley packaged bathing cloths that had a picture of a nurse and an old person on the wrapper. The cloths were always warm, presumably courtesy of a microwave oven. They'd start with my legs, usually, and would wash and dry them with practiced expertise, always sure to first turn on the overhead heat lamp so I wouldn't freeze. (Ventricular devices aren't the same as hearts when it comes to keeping one feeling toasty. They circulate the blood in a continuous flow, rather than with the pulsatile rhythm of natural cardiac function. Without that brio, the blood moves and the oxygen supplies the organs with life, but the vigor is lost and things happen at a minimum. I think I was always freezing, probably to everyone else's annoyance). They would even wash my private parts — sometimes. If they asked me if I would like to do it, I always said yes. If they didn't ask, I didn't offer. I felt like they might as well, I guess. I didn't feel like a person, anyway, so it made sense to just go with it, or so it seemed.

The fanciest part of the whole nighttime bathing operation was the rolling. Somehow, via spatial skills which I do not possess, by my merely rolling (more like being rolled) from side to side and holding onto the bedrails, the nurse at hand was able to wash my back and ass, change my gown, change the damn sheets, and dry me and all of the stuff scrunched under me in the process.

It was so difficult to roll, and let's not even talk about how much effort was required to maintain the roll and hold myself up. I was so weak. I didn't even see how thin and wasted I had become until weeks later, post-transplant, when I finally stood in front of a mirror. I don't think Jeremy saw it either — he did know earlier than I did, though. There was one day when he was helping me adjust an arm with a plethora of IVs and whatnot into the gown, and his face dropped a bit. I think he said, "Oh, my poor girl is so skinny now." Could you just break down into heaving sobs? Somehow, I can't. I get a little watery and frustrated, but then my mind wanders. I was emaciated.

After being washed and medicated, I would literally pray for sleep. Actually, I didn't literally pray. I spoke inside my mind, begging to know why this was happening to me and when I could finally wake up and be back in my apartment with Sedaris and Jeremy and no nightmare.

"I'd almost rather be at work," I would joke to Charlene.

Aside from tooth brushing, and the tender care from the neat and packaging ICU nurses who would roll me up like a sausage, personal hygiene in general seemed sparse. I cannot remember if I once applied deodorant. Unwashed head hair is gross. God bless Charlene, who, to her own incredible horror, amazingly shampooed, conditioned, and combed my hair all while under threat of electrocution — my possible electrocution — as the pumps keeping me alive apparently were never to be allowed to become wet. I really had no idea until afterward how scary it was for her. She says now that she was soaked through with sweat at the end of these occasions. I remember being covered with the many, many towels the nurses, who were just tickled silly that I had such a steady supply of amazing visitors, gave Charlene.

No one who worked there seemed nervous, but they had all been certified in providing critical care to someone being kept alive with extracorporeal heart pumping systems, at least the ones who were assigned to me directly. Maybe they took it for granted that comfort with life support machines is an acquired taste. It is also a skill that must be developed, and that laypeople, even best-of-friends, well-meaning laypeople might be uncomfortable with such a teetery, tangible balance between life and death. Casually telling Charlene that hair washing might result in electrocution might have come off as scarier than it had been intended.

The night I met Charlene must have been Halloween. She was wearing one of those headbands that makes it look like the wearer has funny ears or horns. Hers were Satan ears. My friend Ephraim was there too, a religious Jewish guy who listens to heavy metal and probably doesn't celebrate Halloween. I was happy to meet Mo's then girlfriend and now wife, and was definitely nervous. I usually don't get along with women, probably mostly because I am so insecure. I later learned that she had been nervous to meet me! That's ridiculous. I don't make anyone nervous.

Our initial meeting was pleasant enough, albeit brief, but I think our individual friendship was formalized not more than two weeks later. I happened to walk past the Avenue U subway station in Brooklyn and saw Charlene standing in front, looking annoyed. She was waiting for Mo to pick her up — he was very late — and wondered if I had heard from him. Through calling Lyle, a common friend, from a payphone, I learned that Mo had been hit by a car while jogging and had been taken to the hospital. I told Charlene and she ran into the middle of the street, forgetting we were in Brooklyn, trying to get a cab. I knew there was a car service depot around the corner and led her there. I have a hard time with talking and knowing what to say sometimes, and I don't think we said much as we had no information and were terrified. I felt like I should say something, though, so I apparently turned to her and, something she still makes fun of to this day, quietly asked, "Wanna hug?" More than once Charlene has noted that with all the happenings of friendship, it has been hard to keep straight that I was actually friends with Mo for a long time before she and I met. Should another hair tragedy occur in my life, I will likely insist that Charlene not come near it. Between the head shaving tequila evening (from my pre-celiac disease hair loss episode) which led to another event that involved being accused of having cancer for wearing a ski hat in a sports bar in Shohola, Pennsylvania ("Because no one wears hats here unless they have cancer") and now this horror, she is excused. She probably will always be my Come to the Salon With Me partner, of course.

I remember tilting my head all the way back, salon sink style. Naturally, the pink basin was involved as receptacle, and its matching pink ice pitcher (ice not included) was the pourer of the warm tap water. I would later learn this water had tested positive for legionella, aka Legionnaire's Disease and was the reason for the sign placement warning against showering and tooth brushing, my two favorite luxuries. Or was the legionella uptown at Columbia University Medical Center? I think it may have been both, as they are part of the same hospital system, as is Methodist, come to think of it. You'll recall what I've said about Methodist Hospital. If it had only been at Methodist, I'd guess that poorly-trained residents had infected the water intentionally so they could practice unprofessionally delivering bad news to previously healthy young people. I'd really like to go back there and find those people and tell them what delivering life-changing medical news in such a cruel and insensitive way does to someone. They should know so they can think twice about the impact of their delivery.

A few of these hair washing episodes were all Charlene's nerves could take, and our ritual switched mediums from shampoo, conditioner, and water, to "washless" shampoo.

"Washless" shampoo is pretty grody. It's talcum powder, essentially, and so it wicks away the hair oils, theoretically. It's not so distasteful a product that no one in real life uses it, probably, but I'm not sure I'd be friends with the type of person who might have this stored in his or her bathroom, to be perfectly honest. I'm kind of judgmental like that, but I generally think I mean it in a good-natured, non-hateful kind of style. I thought nothing about this while physically in this predicament, of course, and was thrilled to have a good friend doting on me, thinking nothing of using such a product which results in and enables questionable hygiene.

CHAPTER 11

DOG PEOPLE PROBLEMS

Jeremy

It felt like a year since I had been back in Brooklyn even though it had been less than two days. Our friend Melissa confirmed that she'd picked up Sedaris from the kennel. Sedaris was safe and happy in New Jersey playing with her best friend Gursty. Everything was in order and there was now the thing I had to face, that would repeat itself about 60 more times in the next ten weeks. It was time to go home without my wife. It was heartbreaking for both of us. Joclyn was very supportive. She knew I had to go home and get rest. She understood this would be a long haul, a marathon, and burning myself out would do neither of us any good. But it was still difficult. Joclyn was always so sad about it and always asked for a few more minutes, while I wanted to get it over with and leave because the feeling of guilt was overwhelming. As much as I could intellectually justify going home, emotionally I felt like I was abandoning her. I took a cab that first night. I was in no mood to deal with the subway. I left Joclyn with her phone in her hand so we could be in touch while I was gone. I described the drive home and everything I passed via text. She sucked up every detail wanting more.

Joclyn

Whenever Jeremy left it felt like a huge trauma. Almost like a trained dog — as the loss of so much dignity oftentimes made me feel — I would pick up on cues, smell the air, notice the clock, and fully understand when it was approaching time for him to go home and leave me alone, surrendering custody to the night shift. I would always push for him to stay for another episode of *Dexter*, *The Office*, or another snack from the vending machine. I only briefly considered asking that he stay overnight on a reclining chair.

When the man in the room to my right went home, I was promised a transfer. His room was much bigger, had a table for visitors and piles of crap, and — best of all — came with a folding cot to accommodate an overnight visitor. I got the transfer. When Jeremy stayed over, I practically sobbed with happiness. Imagine being able to spend an overnight in the same room as one's spouse. It was wonderful to not have to have him leave. It was horrible to have to use a bedpan five feet from him. Knowing that he was there didn't make being there any better, or easier, but it made me feel safer, and more able to advocate for myself. I wouldn't have to worry about a call bell unanswered (which honestly did happen very infrequently at Weill Cornell) or about being too alone with my thoughts. Jeremy seemed to sleep better than me on those overnight stays. I'm not sure how, since he later reported that the cot was obnoxiously uncomfortable.

I missed my dog. Jeremy sometimes accused me of thinking more about Sedaris than him. I hope that this wasn't true, considering the person he is, but I think the difference is that I am responsible for Sedaris. Jeremy takes care of me because he is a wonderful person, not because of anything I created or forced. When Jeremy told me that Sedaris had pooped on the floor in the apartment, something that she hadn't done since the third day I had her (except for one time when she was very sick, and another incident involving a chicken parmesan hero) I knew that it was my fault, and that she knew I was so sick and was upset. I wanted to hold her.

CHAPTER 12

REINFORCEMENTS

Jeremy

When I got home, I called my dad and he told me he and Matthew would pick me up in Brooklyn the next morning. This was great news because the train ride to the hospital was long and slow on the weekends, not to mention the long walk from Lexington Avenue down to York Avenue, way over on the east side of Manhattan. This experience helped me understand why living on York Avenue is less expensive than most areas in the city. It's about as far from a train as you can possibly get. The forecast was for light snow, slush, and freezing temperatures, so a lift to the hospital was even more comforting. I continued to text Joclyn to keep her in the loop, anything to help her keep her mind occupied. As the day went on Joclyn was clearly feeling the impact of the operation, and the pain was getting worse. I knew the next couple of days would be rough. I went on the computer and updated Facebook and let on to what was happening for the first time. Most of the people in our lives did not know what was going on. Only our immediate family and some of our closest friends were aware of the dramatic events that had just occurred. I did not have time to call everyone. It was then that I realized I needed to send an email to all of our friends and family. This would at least inform the majority of people in our lives with details a Facebook status update could not offer. I sent out the email and cut and paste the content of it and used Facebook messaging to hit everyone on my "friends" list who was actually a friend. The word was out.

I woke up the next morning to a thin layer of snow, not more than an inch, on the ground. It was barely coming down, so I knew my father would not be bothered by it driving into Brooklyn from New Jersey. He and Matthew arrived at 10:00 a.m. as discussed the night before. I was glad to see some family. They were in shock. I did not know how they would react to the tubes; the thick ones were red because they were pumping blood back and forth from the CentriMag. It was not easy to ignore or put out of your mind. We drove uptown and found parking, grabbed some food, and a Pepsi for Joclyn. When we got into the room Joclyn looked very alert and happy to see the three of us. My father raved how good she looked, and it was great to see that kind of reaction. When I handed Joclyn her Pepsi she pushed it back and told me she did not want it.

Joclyn

The visits from visitors sustained me and kept me from willing myself dead. Jeremy obviously was King Visitor, but the lengths to which others went were just incredible.

My father and brother-in-law Matthew drove up and were in the room when Dr. Horn came in and confirmed that I did have giant cell myocarditis. I understand that their faces aged and altered, but I don't remember witnessing that process as I had a swan catheter in my neck at the time and was unable to turn my head to the left. This became a dark joke between Matthew and me. "What? I can't see you." Perhaps birthing the impression the nurses would do, Matthew was my biggest supporter of "This is so fucked up." We would make eye contact and he would nod vigorously anew each time I reminded the room.

December 3, 1967: According to Wikipedia, the first human heart transplantation was performed on that day in South Africa by Dr. Christiaan Bernard, and the first one in the United States was achieved three days later by Dr. Adrian Kantrowitz at Maimonides Medical Center in Brooklyn. Columbia University Medical Center, where the medical team at Weill Cornell told me I would go for the transplant, has been the pioneering institution as far as making heart transplants real successes, both during the actual transplant surgery and during the aftercare. I took some comfort in this.

In any other era of human existence, I realized, I would not have stood a chance at survival. The anatomical structure of the human heart was studied by the Greeks in the 4th century BC. Its physiological importance was not more completely realized until 600 years later, and it was not until the 19th century where Daniel Hale Williams performed the first successful open-heart surgery at Provident Hospital in Chicago. As recently as 2000, 90 percent of people diagnosed with giant cell myocarditis have either died or received a heart transplant within one year of the diagnosis. I took slightly less comfort in knowing this.

My mother-in-law later came up from Raleigh by train and stayed with Mo's parents in Edgewater, New Jersey. She came every day and "sat" with me, bringing food and company.

Matthew would come again, this time with his wife Madhavi, and they would spend an entire week away from their three children, staying at my apartment with Jeremy, and even spending New Year's Eve with me in the ICU. They brought food for me and Madhavi stayed with me while Matthew provided much relief to Jeremy by getting beer and pizza with him a few times. I'd rather have been part of those times.

CHAPTER 13

NO PEPSI! SNAPPLE!

Jeremy

Joclyn told me she no longer wanted Pepsi because it reminded her of the whole incident two days before. Now she wanted Peach Snapple Iced Tea and only Peach Snapple Iced Tea. She strictly warned me not to bring lemon or raspberry. I promised to get it right and drank the Pepsi myself. Unfortunately Joclyn was in a lot of pain, and she kept telling anyone that would listen that she felt like she got hit by a bus. She told me to fuck off when I asked if she had ever been hit by a bus. I could not help but laugh. She could make me laugh in the worst of times.

As we sat in the room with Joclyn, we tried to help take her mind off her pain. Dr. Horn came into the room. As one of the top cardiologists in the world, her time was highly valued. I told my father to be silent as she filled us in on the results of the biopsy. We were finally going to find out what had caused all this and what the next steps were going to be. "You have giant cell myocarditis," she said. Joclyn and I looked at each other and both said, "I knew it!" She told us that this was an extremely rare disorder, and that she doubted we knew; somehow though, we just knew. Dr. Horn reminded us that this did not alter the overall plan. But there would be a different course of treatment after the heart transplant than there would be if this was a virus and not giant cell myocarditis causing the problem in her heart. I quickly looked at Joclyn before she could speak. I told her I was sorry, but she was going to need a heart transplant. She took it well and admitted that she knew it was heading towards that direction and asked how long I knew. I told her about my talk with Dr. Chen the previous day and wanted to wait to tell her.

Joclyn would still need her next surgery in about ten days to replace the CentriMag with the LVAD, as long as the right side of her heart proved to function well enough on its own. Otherwise, we would get the bigger device which would require a lot more nursing on my part. But because she had giant cell, she would be given a treatment of Cytoxan every ten days — which had been known to tame the disease. This was basically chemotherapy, but not as much as a cancer patient would get. They would continue this treatment after the heart transplant for 6–12 months to stop the giant cell from recurring, as it could still be in the area surrounding the new heart. Joclyn asked if she would be able to run again and Dr. Horn quickly told her she would, just as confidently as Dr. Chen had told her. She told us Joclyn would get the transplant at Columbia University Medical Center in Washington Heights and would live a normal life afterwards. I was relieved that we knew what had caused this. According to Dr. Horn, we had a 75% chance that it would not recur. We were also assured that if it came back, it would not come back as aggressively because Joclyn would be on immunosuppressants. We had a plan. The next step was to keep Joclyn as comfortable as possible for the next 10 days.

I looked over at my father and brother as Dr. Horn finished giving us the news. They looked very down and depleted. While I was glad to have an explanation and was feeling like we had a plan to get through this whole mess after feeling completely helpless, I realized that for my brother and father, who had not endured the past several frightening days, this was shocking news and difficult to accept. I had hit rock bottom the night before the surgery and my mood had only one way to go: up. But Matthew and my father lacked that context. They were still adjusting to the tubes entering and leaving her body. I realized that all of my friends and family may have missed the picture of how grave our situation had been, and how long a road lay ahead of us. I knew I needed a better way to communicate events to everyone, something a little less public than my Facebook account that included over 700 friends, most of whom I did not really know. I told my father and brother that as grim as

Joclyn's diagnosis was, it was good news because it gave us a course of action to follow. They forced a smile and agreed.

One of the recurring themes in this drama was Joclyn's insistence that this was somehow her fault. She maintained there must have been something she could have done to prevent contracting this illness. When Dr. Horn gave us the diagnosis, Joclyn remarked that she herself should have done something sooner to figure out what was happening. Joclyn also questioned the doctors at Methodist for not discovering the disease that was overtaking her heart. Then my brother helped put her mind at ease by bringing up a very valid point. It took an open-heart surgery for them to take a tiny slice of her heart for a biopsy. Are doctors really going to biopsy a person's heart because of flu-like symptoms, or what clearly appears to be a virus? People fill emergency rooms with these symptoms every day. (Although there WAS the test they ran at Methodist a couple of weeks before that provided an opportunity to conduct a biopsy…) But let's be realistic: there were about 45 known cases of giant cell myocarditis in the hospital's database. It is not exactly something a doctor would normally suspect or look for. The fact that this hospital had dealt with patients with giant cell was very fortunate for Joclyn and our hopes for her survival. After that, Joclyn reserved her blame to her parents for a childhood full of stress and aggravation as the catalyst for the disease. I kept my opinion of this philosophy to myself. I thought she was reaching for an explanation, and I felt that there is not always a reason or explanation for everything that happens to us in the world.

Joclyn

We reluctantly watched *Dexter* one night, after about ten minutes of bickering over what to stream, and we immediately fell in love. What a fantastic show that is! We also watched a lot of *The Office*, but that show is really painful after a while. I also will forever associate *The Office* with being in the hospital, but somehow this does not represent my feelings toward *Dexter*.

(I also have horrible associations with Bejeweled Blitz. I played it quite a lot during the week that I was home in between Methodist Hospital and Weill Cornell, and I almost feel like I'm wearing a LifeVest defibrillator accoutrement when playing it. Also, even when playing with a fully functioning heart, it is quite close to impossible to get a really high score when playing it on a laptop. The trackpad is not as agile as an external mouse, I have convinced myself. How do people get scores in the 700,000s? Even with power-ups, I don't think I've ever gotten higher than 200,000.)

I thought I would also never again be able to drink Pepsi or peach-flavored Snapple iced tea, as they were my sustenance for quite a lot of the time, but I can again stomach those as well now. Dr. Chen once suggested that I write a letter to Snapple. I understood what he must have meant, but what would I say to them, really?

Dear Snapple,

Your peach-flavored tea is providing me with a delicious flavor and several minutes of pleasure each day as I lie here, essentially immobile, hoping not to die, but also hoping someone else dies so his or her heart can be harvested and put into my body so at least we both don't die.

Love,
Joclyn

Seriously, right? How would the person feel who opened that letter? Would he be motivated to send me a free case or a booklet filled with coupons? How would that have improved my life, really? Everyone who came to visit me in the hospital brought peach-flavored Snapple, both diet and regular, at some point. All of the windowsills and available surfaces were covered with sugary beverages, various gourmet nonperishable products from Trader Joe's, and two incentive spirometers (those blue plastic tubes attached to a base with a little ball inside that goes up when blown into to try and prevent pneumonia) which had each hit the floor at least twice but so remained because I kept forgetting to tell anyone. Hospital floors don't belong in the mouths of the immune-suppressed.

CHAPTER 14

CYTOXAN AND CARDIAC PRETZELS

Jeremy

My phone rang and it was Uncle Michael and Aunt Susan; they would be visiting the next day. Joclyn always loves spending time with her uncle and aunt and I was grateful they would be arriving shortly. My family would be heading back to North Carolina the next day, but Matthew was already planning on returning with his wife Madhavi for the holidays. Their kids would stay with my parents. I was hoping Joclyn would be coming home about that time with her LVAD device. Then Matthew again addressed the issue of communicating what was happening to our closest friends and family. Madhavi was ready to set up a CaringBridge account. CaringBridge is a website that might be best explained as a Facebook for very sick people, and it would allow us to update everyone concerned about Joclyn and her condition. It would also allow people to post messages to her offering encouragement. I told him it sounded great and would figure that all out soon. Matthew and my father left to go back to New Jersey and told me they would see me in the morning. I stayed with Joclyn until midnight and took a cab home.

When I got home I went right to sleep and waited for my ride to the hospital the next morning, again in a light snow shower. We found parking, and my father and brother went to get some breakfast while I hurried into the hospital. Joclyn was up when I got there and looking better than the day before. I noticed that she was not pushing the pain button as much, and was a lot more alert than the previous day. After a few hours of hanging out, Joclyn's aunt and uncle arrived. We had a packed room with lots of family and our spirits were high.

Uncle Michael handed me a giant canister of big pretzels. Always ready to eat, Matthew and I popped it open and found the saltiest pretzels known to mankind. They were covered in that thick white salt people use on their sidewalks to melt ice. I announced they were cardiac pretzels, and noted the irony of being in a cardiac intensive care unit. We each ate one pretzel and had to stop. The nice thing was those pretzels lasted six weeks as few people could eat them. There were moments of desperation when I was glad I had those pretzels. And every once in a while I was able to pull off some of the salt and feed it to my salt-starved wife. She loves to eat the salt off of pretzels, since her Celiac disease prevents her from eating the actual pretzel.

Joclyn

The rheumatologist was a nice man, though I am not exactly sure of what his role was. He was called in specifically because of my curious history of autoimmune disorders. He seemed genuinely concerned with me as a person, which was not always the norm with the supporting cast of medical professionals who would come in and stare at me periodically. On days he wasn't feeling well, he would only stand at the doorway and wave, holding a mask over his mouth and blowing kisses. He had thinning red hair and a beard; I don't remember him as overweight or very much of any kind of stereotype, but he did come off as jolly, but not in a shopping mall Santa kind of way. I looked forward to his visits.

He almost always arrived with a woman at his side, someone whose name I could never remember, and who in my mind I'd decided was his assistant, though people kept telling me she was a doctor also. She was a lot smaller than him and seemed to look to him to do most of the talking. Maybe I also just don't like women, usually. I called her, in my mind, Assistant Dr. So-and-So.

The two of them introduced me to Cytoxan, a chemotherapeutic agent that was somehow believed to slow the progression of giant cell myocarditis. A special nurse from oncology would come to administer it each time, and she wore gloves. I mean, everyone wore gloves, but she (the various shes) made a special point of wearing gloves. I felt positive about Cytoxan. It seemed quite toxic. Cleverly named drug, too. Ha. Seriously. The point was never to eradicate the giant cell; I'd already surrendered (somewhat) to understanding that this was impossible, but I guess it was rather to slow its progression, "buying time" until a new heart came. I don't really understand this effort to maintain my "native" heart to this day, though, since Dr. Chen and Dr. Horn and Neshama the LVAD specialist and others did say again and again that the machines were my heart, and my heart was just sitting there, but post-transplant I would endure nine months of much higher doses of Cytoxan every three weeks (on an outpatient basis) because Columbia has found that this prevents giant cell from returning and destroying the new, transplanted heart. Oh, right. There's a 25% chance that giant cell will return, although the theory is that because heart transplant recipients are on immunosuppressive medication, it returns less aggressively and is detected earlier, because people like me are routinely monitored for its return, along with regular checks for rejection. A larger n, or a greater number of observations of cases of giant cell, would ease the burden of prediction, but odds thus far were not much in my favor, so perhaps the not knowing is easier.

While not a full chemotherapy regimen, it did knock the crap out of me. If I'd had any responsibilities beyond lying in a hospital bed and trying not to die, I may not have been able to organize myself to complete any expectations beyond just that. Usually, while in the hospital, I would feel a bit nauseous from the Cytoxan, although this particular brand of nausea was practically impossible to differentiate from the baseline nausea that followed me from start to finish, and didn't vanish until I was at home eating a Jeremy-prepared tuna sandwich. (Intravenous Zofran? Feh. How about just an environment devoid of recycled air and vile aromas and horrifically prepared meals?)

CHAPTER 15

SEPARATION ANXIETY

Jeremy

My father and brother left and headed back to North Carolina. Joclyn's mother and her husband Jay replaced them. Our closest friends Mo and Charlene dropped in as well. I actually had to manage the traffic of visitors, but this made getting through the day much easier for both of us. Apart from managing visiting traffic, I had to finish a paper for my graduate class as well. I was determined to keep up with my graduate classes as the master's degree I was working on was mandatory in order to continue as a teacher for the New York City Department of Education. The good news was that the term was almost over and I would not have class again until early February. It was a very busy and action-packed day. It was not long before everyone was gone and it was just Joclyn and I again with our thoughts. This was a particularly difficult evening because I had to return to work the next day. We decided it was best I conserve as many sick days as possible for the days following Joclyn's major surgeries.

Joclyn cried when I left that night. I cried after I left. I could not stay that much past 10:00 p.m. and be effective the following day. I had to go home and get enough sleep each night so I could endure. While this made sense, it did not help with the guilt of leaving her alone in the hospital. The one thing that made all this bearable was the great nursing staff at Weill Cornell. I do not know if we would have made it through it all without their kindness and professionalism. They were well trained and well managed. They played a big role in our daily life while we were there, and we will never forget them. I was well aware of each nurse in charge of Joclyn when I left the hospital, and she would text me who was assigned to her the next morning.

Joclyn

Even my parents visited. Before and after. Not during, though. My mother not only did not come to the hospital on the occasion of a perfect heart match having been found, and my chest being sawed open for a fourth time, but she actually went to work in the morning. I know now that it was the best she could do. I understand that my father came later on in the morning. My surgery had been scheduled to begin at 2 a.m. My parents did generally visit separately, but that they came with any degree of frequency was surprising in a way. Their support was much needed and appreciated.

Sometimes I blame my parents, seriously. I don't know if this makes me *seem* crazy, or *actually* crazy, but I think that if my childhood had been less stressful, I would not have developed such an awful autoimmune disorder. Disorders. Stress doesn't cause things to appear out of thin air, of course, but it certainly doesn't help, and it certainly does aggravate what's already there.

When I was nine, all I wanted as a present for any kind of occasion was a Nintendo Entertainment System. When I was about to turn ten, my life savings had accumulated to about $110, mostly in singles, some quarters, and all of it in my closet in a little red safe, the kind with the built-in combination lock. I trustingly gave it all to my father and begged him to go to Toys R Us and buy me a Nintendo. He said he would, but when he came home with it one evening, whistling Happy Birthday as he came in the door, my mother said, "Uh, no. You're bringing that back tomorrow. And she's not opening it." I never even left my room. I listened from underneath my desk. And he never gave me my money back.

Also, my mother used to trick me into getting haircuts that made me look like a boy. I don't know why. It was so mean. She dressed me like a boy until I started buying my own clothes.

Stress consumed me all through high school as my parents began stealing my mail so I couldn't go to any college besides Brooklyn College. It dominated every conversation. They would whisper about it constantly as though I couldn't hear them. I was making daily, secret collect calls to my aunt for advice and staying very late at school talking with whichever of my favorite teachers were around for moral support. It stole my breath living like that, always tasting tension. I enrolled in 7:30 classes just to be around people who didn't make me feel like that.

In short, these are some examples of the stress that I occasionally blame for my unfair medical history. I know that everyone has had their own upsetting experiences, but I still cannot help but think that there must be a reason for my becoming so ill. Autoimmune disorders, in particular, have little documented rhyme or reason.

CHAPTER 16

FIRST!

Jeremy

When I got home from the hospital there was an email from Madhavi, my sister-in-law, which provided the link to the CaringBridge site she set up. Because I wanted administrative control of the site, she gave me the password and agreed to only post messages that I approved. I was very anal about giving out accurate information to our family and friends, and medical information is easy to miscommunicate when it gets passed through multiple people. The one issue I wanted to address was the high volume of visitors on the weekends. I wanted to make sure people did not come and end up in a waiting room their whole visit. So my first post was actually put up by Madhavi, which I dictated to her over the phone:

> Please DO NOT call or visit unexpectedly.
>
> Please contact Jeremy via email to set up a time to call or visit.
>
> Joclyn needs her rest as much as she needs your well wishes and Jeremy needs to be focused on supporting her.

Now that I was back home, I logged in and realized I should explain what was happening before sharing the link with the outside world. This is what I came up with:

Joclyn had open-heart surgery on Thursday.

They put in a device called a VAD to basically take over the work usually performed by the heart. They needed to do this because her heart was not strong enough to supply her organs with appropriate blood supply. Her kidneys were failing and on Thursday morning she was running out of time. Because of this temporary device, her organs are now fine. Her kidneys are back to normal. Her blood flow is strong. However, her heart is damaged and will not recover.

On December 14th Joclyn will undergo her next surgery to remove the device and insert a smaller device that allows her to go home. This VAD is intended to be a bridge to keep her alive and functioning until she will have a heart transplant. As scary as that sounds, that surgery is no more dangerous than the one she had on Thursday, when her heart and organs were under so much duress.

Her response to the first surgery is leaving the Doctors very optimistic and confident about the next 2. She is Type A blood, which is the best to be when you are waiting for a heart, it may happen in as little as two months. We have the #1 Cardiologist in the country (Dr. Horn) overseeing all this. the transplant will take place at Columbia Pres, which is the best hospital for a heart transplant. If all goes to plan, Joclyn should be resuming her normal active life within a year from now. It will be a hard road, but with all the support we are getting, we are confident it will come to be.

Thanks for all the best wishes, and if you would like to talk you can email me first via email and we can work out the best time to speak.

Thanks again for all the support.

Best regards,
Jeremy

Returning to work on a Monday is never fun. Returning to work on a Monday when your wife is in the hospital recovering from open-heart surgery sucks. The whole thing happened so quickly, seeing the reactions of my coworkers brought me back to the reality of how shocking and scary the whole situation was. The questions people asked repeatedly all week were "How are you doing it? How are you getting through all of this?" These questions became a recurring theme in my life and the answer changed during this process a few times. At this point my answer was simple. "I don't know." The reason I didn't know was that this crisis had risen so quickly, and this was the first day I was back at work. I had yet to do anything to get through anything. I was shell-shocked and terrified of my phone. I worried that at any second bad news would come streaming in that would dash all hope of seeing my wife healthy again. The teachers I worked with were very supportive and offered to help in any way possible. My principal was incredibly supportive and told me to take off whenever I needed to and not worry. Work ended up being a positive distraction.

After work, I would start a routine that I would grow quite used to over the next sixty days. Again, I was fortunate that aside for some final papers I wrote at Joclyn's bedside, I would not have any graduate classes until early February. So my day started at 5:45 a.m. I woke up and left for work by 6:30. I would usually be at work in 15 minutes as long as I avoided getting stuck behind a garbage truck on a one-way street. By 7:00, I was in the teachers' lounge planning my activities for the day, or making some modifications to the lessons prepared by my co-teachers. Classes would start at 8:00 and I was usually kept busy throughout the day.

After the last bell rang I would run for my car and drive home. At home I would prepare some kind of gluten-free meal for Joclyn, and take the train into the city towards the hospital. I would later switch to driving to the hospital when I discovered an area I could park the car. I would usually get to Joclyn's room by 5:00 p.m. She would always light up when I walked in and it was like both of our days had actually started. At first, we kept ourselves busy talking about how shocked we were that this was happening. We were now a bit under two weeks until the next operation that would hopefully allow us to go home with an LVAD device. While we waited for December 14th, there were no major developments. The only activity that was significant was a PET scan to check the status of the disease in Joclyn's body. I do not remember much about how it came about, but this is how I updated everyone on CaringBridge:

> Joclyn got her results from the PET scan. This was a test to see if the autoimmune disorder was still attacking her heart and/or other organs. It was one of our big concerns because if it was, well, it takes a while to get a new heart so you do the math. We got very good news. Apparently the immune disorder is well under control from the medication, no sign of it anywhere including her heart. This means they can move forward with the surgery on Monday to implement the smaller device that lets Joclyn go home while we wait for the new heart. While we have 2 major operations to go, the immediate threat and worry has been contained. Today is a good day. Thanks for all of your thoughts, well wishes, prayers, and love.
>
> Jeremy K.

What I will never understand is how a test like this can be so misleading. We were convinced the disease was out of her system because of this test, and we would find out later this was completely false. Maybe it did not show up because of the Cytoxan they had pumped into Joclyn's system a couple of days before the test. The Cytoxan, again, is chemotherapy and may have temporarily halted the disease, creating a very misleading result. Joclyn was already on anti-nausea medication so she did not notice the effects of the chemo at first. Like most of the procedures Joclyn had done, and would do, we noted how getting treatments of chemo would easily be a huge deal in almost any other situation, but with Joclyn it was barely a footnote to everything else in our lives. To us, it was just another bag of medication they were pumping into her body via one of the tubes going into her system.

Joclyn

CaringBridge is a web service where profiles can be created for sick people. There is a "journal" section, a "guestbook" section, and a "tribute" section where visitors can make monetary contributions to some kind of charitable organization in the sick person's name. My sister-in-law Madhavi set one up for me. She also brought me homemade chicken and rice, and painted the toenails of my swollen, heart-failured feet a couple of times. She has a reasonably acceptable poker face when on her hands and knees in a cardiac ICU.

All of my visitors had poker faces. My friend Heather, while painting my fingernails, looked up at me and casually asked if she should skip the finger that had blood on it.

CaringBridge was a rather big part of my institutional company. Jeremy used to read the guestbook entries to me every few days. I was never big on prayer, per se, but word really gets around, and hearing that some random Baptist group was saying special things just for me, even though my only connection to them was that one of their members lives a few houses down from Jeremy's parents in Raleigh, was enormously helpful. My stock response to hearing of minyanim, prayer circles, karma shapes, and lists was, "I'll take it." I do attribute a lot of my health success to all of the thoughts, prayers, and karma. There was a pretty big study in a real medical journal that suggested that people for whom prayers were said had better outcomes, even if they were unaware they'd been prayed for, than people who weren't the objects of prayer. [Indian J Psychiatry. 2009 Oct–Dec; 51(4): 247–253. Prayer and healing: A medical and scientific perspective on randomized controlled trials] Whatever works, even if it seems unlikely, even for a skeptic. When one's health and safety are in immediate peril, and when desperation arrives, the need for data and rationality goes out the window. "There are no atheists in foxholes." This is how otherwise intelligent people get roped into paying for unlikely, nonsensical cures, but that's not what prayer is.

It would have been nice if all of that energy had been focused prior to the catastrophic disease process, but everyone is usually pretty busy, even people who often pray, I think. Not that I'm blaming the universe for my illness, of course. As I've already explained, I blame my parents. But anyway, here I am.

And here we are. Rereading the CaringBridge journal entries detailing my medical and mental state throughout my hospitalization along with the guestbook entries from friends, families, and strangers is a little bit upsetting, believe it or not!

Exhibit A:

SUNDAY, DECEMBER 6, 2009 7:01 PM, EST

Please DO NOT call or visit unexpectedly.

Please contact Jeremy via email to set up a time to call or visit.

Joclyn needs her rest as much as she needs your well wishes and Jeremy needs to be focused on supporting her.

To me, this reads to be a dying request, or perhaps the disclaimer at the entrance to a haunted house.

The alter ego to the bad news was the peppy commentary left in the guestbook section.

Exhibit B:

SUNDAY, DECEMBER 6, 2009 8:07 PM, EST

Yay! I'm the first one to write in Joclyn's journal!

Madi Krevat

Exhibit C:

SUNDAY, DECEMBER 6, 2009 7:46 PM, EST

Joclyn had open-heart surgery on Thursday.

Jeremy explained everything that had been going on, delivering the grim news, and friends, family, and prayerful strangers provided the relief and support.

I also kept a personal journal, empty pages courtesy of Mo and Charlene. That record also became important as it was necessary for me to communicate via writing for much of the time, as being intubated and extubated so many times left me voiceless, or, as my friend Jenny said, left me sounding like Lauren Bacall.

The dates don't match up exactly, as I wasn't always in a state to write, to say the least, but here is my first entry.

Exhibit D:

12/20/09

Charlene got this journal for me probably weeks ago at this point, and I think I can finally focus enough to write at least one or two complete sentences. This is so fucked up; I don't even have the words to speak about it somewhat intelligently.

Ed. note: Of note is that I had the wherewithal to make proper use of a semicolon.

11:45 pm

All in all a good day as far as being trapped in the ICU goes. Jeremy made me yummy tuna and Mo and C visited and Char washed and braided my hair. Shitting is such a huge deal/ordeal it may be the worst part of this as far as mental health goes. I hit a "had enough" wall today as well. The resident whose name I can't remember pretty much insisted I take Xanax, which I did. Now my eyes are X-ing. (X was hours ago, though.)

Ed. note: X was hours ago probably means Xanax was hours ago.

This is the matching CaringBridge journal entry:

SUNDAY, DECEMBER 20, 2009 4:58 PM, EST

Hey Everyone,

So today was a lot more comfortable for Joclyn. While the drainage tube remains in, it has done a great job making her feel better as her lungs are free of most fluids. We are still on schedule for Tuesday to have the big pump removed. They were talking about 7–10 days to go home after surgery if all goes well. That gives us hope for New Year's Eve at home. We will be ok with celebrating at the hospital if needed though.

So the highlight of the day was Charlene coming and washing Joclyn's hair. Joclyn was smiling the whole time. She also ate the tuna on gluten-free bread I made for her. Right now she is eating Trader Joe's Fruit Jellies as I type this. She likes the red ones, but they give very few red ones. Why is that?

Anyhow, she looks really good and strong, and is looking ready to go in and get this last thing done to go home and wait for that phone call. We will certainly make the most of the time before that call, lots of time with friends, walks with the dog, and some time for her to write, read, and catch up on TV. She can't wait to see what happened on The Amazing Race, and will Adam from Man vs Food, be able to eat a 3-meter bratwurst with 2 significant sides? Let's not tell her how he did!

Anyhow, she loves and appreciates all your messages and wants you all to know she appreciates all of your good thoughts and vibes. We are really looking forward to going back to places like D.C. and NC, and eating in our favorite Indian, Wings, and Hot Dog places. A trip to Smallwood is also anticipated for some nice relaxation time doing crosswords and making fun of the shoppers in the local Walmart.

Joclyn's humble husband,
Jeremy K.

CHAPTER 17

CAN YOU THROW ME A FREAKIN' BONE?

Jeremy

Two days before Joclyn's next surgery, my mother came to visit us. She stayed in Edgewater with Stan and Eileen, who had been our neighbors in Brooklyn when I was growing up. They are also Mo's parents. I think my friendship with Mo is the biggest factor in my mother staying so close to Eileen. While living 500 miles apart, they continue to stay in touch and offer support to each other as their lives require it. Mo and I get to see each other a lot more often as we live in the same city. During this ordeal, I had longed to take Joclyn to the Lakeside Lounge on the Lower East Side of Manhattan to see Mo and Charlene's band, Spanking Charlene, bring down the house with their awesome music.

It was great that Stan and Eileen were there to take my mother in, as it would have been impossible for me to host her at my place in Brooklyn. Joclyn was happy to have my mother visit. They had grown close over the past couple of years, and my mother would be able to keep Joclyn company during the day. Aside from a couple of lunches in the city with old friends, she did just that. Unfortunately, there was the usual drama that always follows my mother around, including the bag full of Trader Joe's goodies she left on a city bus because she was so stressed about our whole ordeal. I felt bad that my mother was so upset about a few groceries. I emphasized to her that being around to support us was a lot more important. My mother loves to go the extra mile to make the people she loves happy, so I know it still bothers her to this day.

A visit from my mother also meant a lot of jewelry for people. In this case, it was the nurses who were the lucky recipients of handmade earrings and bracelets. I gave Derrick a Coach wallet, which I saw no reason to add to the pile of unused wallets I've received as gifts from my mother. Even though I have insisted to my mother that I use a money clip, my mother is always buying me wallets from Coach. She is too generous for her own good sometimes. I think she sees money clips as cheap and wants me to have better. Anyway, it was great to give out gifts to these incredible people who were doing such a great job taking care of Joclyn. Even Neshama got some earrings in exchange for information about growing up in Israel.

As we got closer to the insertion of the LVAD, visits from Neshama became more frequent. It was time for me to start my training, and prove that I could take care of Joclyn at home while we waited for a heart. The first lesson involved putting on sterile gloves. Neshama warned me about the dangers of contaminating the gloves. She warned me that failing to sterilize the gloves properly could lead to a dangerous infection that could harm Joclyn. As she handed me a user manual for the LVAD, she warned, "I am tough and will not let her come home with you if you do not know this inside and out." This warning was effective. I not only read the manual, but asked Joclyn to quiz me on its contents many times in case I was given a pop quiz.

During a visit with Marc, and Joclyn's younger sister Rachel, Neshama came in to give us more details about the LVAD. She began to warn us about the dangers of the device if Joclyn was put in certain situations. "If you crash the car, she will die." I promised we would limit our time in the car. "If you slam on the brakes too hard you can kill her." I promised not to slam the brakes. "You must make sure you change the batteries before they die, or she will die." I swore that I would not take her too far away from the house and would make sure we had fresh batteries with us at all times. "Oh no. You can go wherever you like, just don't crash the car, slam on the brakes, or let the batteries die." She proceeded to lecture Marc and Rachel about the dangers that lay ahead and how likely it was that something could go horribly wrong. After she left, Rachel walked away looking a bit pale, and maybe even a shade of green. Marc came over to me and asked what was up with "Dr. Gloom-and-Doom." I started to laugh. This intimidating woman that was scaring the life out of me was now the butt of our jokes. Even Joclyn was laughing about it. Marc complained "My daughter is about to have another open-heart surgery, and needs a heart transplant. Can you throw me a freaking bone?" I joined in. "If the dog barks too loud, she is dead." Marc added, "If she sneezes, she is dead." Neshama is not a doctor, but Dr. Gloom-and-Doom, she certainly was.

Her gloom-and-doom attitude did not stop there. Every once in awhile she would join another physician's assistant and look at Joclyn's heart via some kind of portable X-ray machine. We could not help but hear her whisper things like "the left side of the heart is completely dead." Normally it would be hard to hear what a person was saying when they were making it a point to whisper. But she seemed to have a whisper louder than a Yankee fan watching a playoff game against the Red Sox. I could not help but wonder if she enjoyed having us hear how dead Joclyn's heart was, and how it lacked any signs of life. This was no secret at this point, since they were no longer able to feel a pulse. Doctors and nurses, because they could not monitor Joclyn's pulse, used a device called a Doppler. With a Doppler, medical staff could be sure the LVAD was pumping blood to the vital areas of her body. The Doppler is a very old device. It actually had a speaker that would blast out the sound for all of us to hear. There were some scary moments where it seemed to take forever for them to get it to work and confirm her blood was flowing.

The time for the second surgery had arrived. We were not very optimistic that Joclyn's heart had recovered enough for the doctors to put in an LVAD. Although, if it had, we would be home around December 27th in time for New Year's Eve. Because I dreaded the possibility of the larger machine, I tried not to think about it, even though Neshama's whispered remarks made it sound likely we would end up with it. This would require more training. I was sure Neshama would add about 50 more ways I could be responsible for the death of my wife. Dr. Chen assured me that the first open-heart surgery was much more life-threatening than this upcoming surgery. Joclyn was not in the state of emergency she was two weeks ago. But with any surgery, particularly open-heart surgery, there is always significant risk. Joclyn was again more concerned about waking up during the surgery. Even though, clearly, this did not happen during the first surgery as I and the surgeons assured her, her fear of it was just as strong this time around. I had to remind myself not to tell her she was being ridiculous, and calmly reassure her that they would not let her wake up on the operating table. Soon the surgical team came to bring her downstairs. I was left alone with my mother. We headed to the same pub Marc and I had visited during the first surgery. I think Marc went with us as well, but those few hours have since become a blur to me.

Joclyn

Heart failure and bedpans can make you crazy, so they gave me antipsychotic medication. The recurring yellow things crawling my walls disappeared, and I was finally able to sleep. ICU psychosis is real, too, and so of course I developed that one as well.

I don't know when it started to happen, but at some point I realized that I had lost all of my strength as well as a frightening amount of weight. I was in good shape to begin with. As I was shimmying from stretcher to operating table for my possible CentriMag removal surgery (open-heart surgery number two), I commented aloud that this was the most exercise I had had in weeks. It was hard, and I needed help. Everyone laughed. I always make people laugh. I'm still not sure if they were actually listening.

The nurses at Weill Cornell were so fantastic, and it worked out perfectly that Sandra Krevat, my mother-in-law, makes jewelry as a hobby. She gave us bags and bags of necklaces, earrings, and bracelets to distribute to the team. ("For your girlfriend, or your mom," we told nurses like JoJo.) Derrick the nurse was extra-special, and so we gave him an "extra" Coach wallet. (Ed. note: Jeremy's mom has generously given him many wallets over the years.) I think we gave Arvin a matching set of things to give to his girlfriend; he was superb in care as well, going so far beyond what I would have expected from any nurse. He chatted with me about the *Fables* graphic novels that Melissa brought, and talked about his life a bit: his girlfriend, his original career choice that moved him to study at the School of Visual Arts. If he is half as good an artist as he is a nurse, his drawings should be hanging in galleries all over the world. I mean that. I was fascinated by his career change, silently wishing to trade places with him, and making a pledge with myself that I would at least consider being an OT who works with cardiac intensive care patients.

CHAPTER 18

YOU CAN'T GO HOME WITH A CENTRIMAG

Jeremy

I remember Dr. Chen coming into the waiting room and giving me his very familiar smile as he approached. This meant that Joclyn was okay. Now that I had established she was alive, I wanted to know the results of the surgery. I hoped he would tell me they were able to put in the LVAD. It turned out to be neither of the options I had expected. They did insert the LVAD, but they left the CentriMag connected to the right side of her heart. Dr. Chen explained that they felt the right side of the heart would recover enough to rely only on the LVAD, but wanted to give it a bit more time. I quickly asked how long it would be until they disconnected the CentriMag. He estimated another week. This was sad news, as it meant another operation for Joclyn. Dr. Chen saw the look on my face. He assured me it would be a quick and easy procedure. If it was done on December 22nd, there was still hope of getting her home by New Year's Eve. I looked over at Marc and my mother, and they shrugged their shoulders showing the same feeling of relief and frustration that I felt. It is hard to say it was good news, but Joclyn survived another open-heart surgery, so you can't call it bad news either.

I got to see Joclyn very briefly before I left the hospital for home. I was sad that she would wake up and I would not be there. My mother would be there the next morning to keep her company while I was at work. Since the surgery was a success, and my mother was in town, we determined that I could return to work and preserve a sick day. I drove home thinking about how Joclyn was going to feel when she woke up and saw the CentriMag connected to her. That machine was a symbol of being stuck in the hospital with no way to come home. It prevented her from freely moving around and kept her from walking more than a few feet with the physical and occupational therapist a few times a week. I took a deep breath when I thought about another 14–17 days in the hospital. I was grateful we were getting closer to the holiday break. At least I could be with her, over the holiday break, from morning to night for ten straight days.

Joclyn

I woke up with the CentriMag AND an LVAD, instead of just an LVAD, and there went the possibility of going home anytime soon. The right side of my heart had not recovered enough for safe CentriMag removal, and so it remained in my chest. Two devices controlling my blood circulation, neither of which is my actual heart, does not create a situation easily surpassable in fucked-up-ness. Dr. Chen explained that the right side of my heart would hopefully continue to recover, and that perhaps in another week or two I would have another (open-heart) surgery to (finally) remove the CentriMag.

I just wanted to go home. I asked Jeremy if he would trade places with me for just 24 hours, and that I promised I would come right back to the ICU. He insisted that he would if he could.

CHAPTER 19

RED COOLERS: NOT JUST FOR BEER

Jeremy

The next morning, I woke up at my usual time and got into work at 6:45. I was happy not to hear from the hospital. That indicated everything was alright. I had just settled into a seat by a computer in the teachers' lounge when my cell phone started to ring. I looked at the caller ID and saw it was the hospital. I felt a knife go in my stomach and slowly twist. I swallowed hard and picked up the phone and answered "hello?" in a very weak voice. "Mr. Krevat I am calling about your wife. We are trying to save her life." I looked at the phone like it bit me and yelled back: "What? She was fine last night, what is happening?" She hesitated and yelled something at someone near her. "Mr. Krevat, your wife has internal bleeding and she wants you to come to the hospital right away." I started to panic as I found myself back in a place I thought I'd escaped. I was back to thinking I was going to lose Joclyn. "Is she going to be okay? What are you doing to help her?" There was another two-second pause that seemed like two hours. Then a yell, "We are trying to save her life!" I told her I was coming right away. Unlike my conversation with Dr. Bender ten days before, I decided telling her to tell Joclyn I loved her would be fruitless. This caller did not seem the type that would relay that message.

I grabbed my bag and thought about the fastest way to the hospital. I decided it was still early enough to avoid major traffic by car. As I ran down the hall trying to decide how to let my principal know I would not be at work today, I saw my friend John. John is a caring and attentive person, so the minute he looked at my face he knew that something had gone wrong. I started to explain that I needed to let Rebecca (our principal) know that I had to leave, but before I could finish John hollered, "just go!" I turned and was down three flights of stairs in about ten seconds. I flew out the door into the parking lot and ran towards my car. It occurred to me that teachers were arriving to work and I could get hit by a car due to the hurried, careless way I ran out of the building. But I could not slow down. I drove out of the parking lot and was on my way no more than 30 seconds after my encounter with John. I began the most reckless drive of my life. It was as if there was no other car or pedestrian on the streets. I was back to driving like a New York City taxi driver. I might be driving to see my wife one last time before I lost her. I tried to calm myself down, but it was impossible.

I was lucky that rush hour hadn't begun. I am not sure I would have stayed sane if I got stuck in traffic. I managed to make it to the Upper East Side in one piece and drove to the parking lot with which I had become so familiar over the preceding weeks. I parked and ran full speed towards the entrance of the hospital. As I ran, my phone rung. It was my mother. I must have called her at some point because she told me she was getting ready and heading right over. I told her I would see her soon and headed to the elevator. As I was waiting for it my phone rang again and the caller ID made it clear it was the hospital calling again, the hospital I was standing in. I answered the phone thinking it might be a doctor telling me they did all they could do but Joclyn had lost too much blood. My hand was shaking. "Mr. Krevat?" A man with a southern and familiar accent asked. "I am a resident surgeon that works with Dr. Chen. Are you close by?" I told him I was downstairs and on my way up; my voice was shaking. He must have heard it because he assured me they would take good care of Joclyn and that he would talk to me in a few minutes. I was just glad he was not telling me the news I had feared the most.

When I got to the correct floor and was heading towards Joclyn's room, I was trailing behind two nurses carrying a red cooler marked "Human Blood." I felt like I was in a worsening nightmare. I wished I could wake up. As I suspected, they led me right to my wife's room. The blood was for her. The surgeon on the phone was there and greeted me with a warm smile. I must have been white as a ghost because he grabbed me and looked me in the eye assuring me he was going to take good care of her. His accent sounded familiar for a reason. I can recognize a North Carolina accent anywhere. I lived there for two years. It is the home of my parents and brother. I will always consider North Carolina one of my homes. It's odd and makes no sense, but this doctor's North Carolina origins put me at ease. I sensed immediately that he had attended Duke, and that reinforced my confidence in him. I asked him what was going to happen. He was very relaxed considering the nurses were running around in a frenzy. "Mr. Krevat, this is not uncommon. We are going to open her back up and find the source of the bleeding, and she will be okay."

I went to Joclyn's side and she was semi-conscious. I grabbed her hand and she squeezed my hand to show that she was aware I was there. I told her she was going to be okay, and she should just relax. One of our favorite nurses, Derrick, was in the room. He was very focused on his job at that moment. It was the most serious I had ever seen him. He only acknowledged me with a stare and a nod. I knew that he cared about Joclyn, and that he was compassionate where she was concerned. Derrick told me that they would be taking her down for surgery in a few minutes. Joclyn was muttering for me. She told me she was scared. I started to cry because I could not imagine what she was feeling. I took a deep breath and got control of myself before leaning over and telling her she was fine, and this would all be over soon. I told her she had nothing to fear. She squeezed my hand letting me know that she heard me. I told her I would have lots of Peach Snapple Iced Tea ready when she woke up. A few minutes later they wheeled her away. The surgeon grabbed my shoulder and promised me Joclyn would be fine. I left for the waiting room, exhausted and drained.

After about 30 minutes my mother walked in. I was trying not to cry as I sat with my face buried in my hands. My mother told me it was going to be okay. We sat quietly as we waited. She asked me if there was anything to eat because she ran over without eating. I was not upset that she asked for food at a time like this; it gave me something to do. I went to the room to get her some of the snacks we had accumulated on the windowsill. As I walked into the now empty room, it reflected how I felt on the inside. I was completely empty. The other two surgeries were planned. I had time to prepare, and understood how they would help my wife recover. This was different: the only objective of this surgery was to save her life. She was bleeding internally, and it needed to be stopped. I watched them fill my wife with three bags of blood in the short time I was with her that morning. I sat there wondering what would happen if they simply could not stop the bleeding inside of her. I wished I could be in the operating room just in case she didn't make it. I did not want her to be alone if she died.

Minutes turned into two hours as we sat there in the waiting room. Finally, I looked up and saw Dr. Chen walking towards us. He flashed me a quick smile which came over me like a flow of warmth and comfort I had never experienced before in my life. I knew at that moment that Joclyn had dodged another bullet. Joclyn's bleeding had stopped. Dr. Chen was actually relieved that he had been able to open her up again and clean her up more thoroughly. He said he was very confident she was out of danger, and that she would be fine. I called Marc to let him know his daughter was okay. He had left work and was on his way. When I called him he was a few blocks away; he was silent when I told him she was alive and well. There was a pause that I would later find out was Marc leaning against a building unable to stand while he tried to catch his breath. "Thank God" was all he could muster. He would be upstairs in a few minutes. I could tell he was crying and I realized once again how close we had come to losing her.

Joclyn

I also had an emergency surgery to stop internal bleeding. This was in between open-heart surgery numbers two and three. I remember being really sleepy; I remember seeing bags of blood hanging everywhere — how did they know my blood type? — and I also remember a nurse telling me to shut up and asking if I wanted to die when I repeatedly tried to ask for something to drink.

CHAPTER 20

FORGET THE OXYGEN! GIVE ME A SNAPPLE!

Jeremy

A couple of hours passed while we hung out in the waiting room waiting for the okay to visit Joclyn. Finally, one of the nurses came out to let us know we could go back to the room and see her. When I entered the room, she was awake with the breathing tube still in her mouth. She looked at me and I gave her a nod and told her how proud of her I was for fighting so hard to survive. She still looked scared. I assured her she was fine and was going to be all right. She motioned for me to come over, unable to speak to me because of the breathing tube still in her. I was horrified to see the question "Am I going to die?" written on her notepad. I was very upset that Joclyn was feeling this way. Once again I promised her she was going to be okay. This time I actually believed it. Joclyn would later tell me this episode was the one she was most convinced would kill her. She believed she was dying. Over the next few days, I would be committed to helping her deal with that experience as best as possible in order to maintain her sanity.

The next objective was to get the breathing tube removed from her throat. This required Joclyn to pass breathing tests that demonstrated her capacity to deliver adequate oxygen to her body without a machine assisting her. In the meantime, a nurse gave me a stick with a little sponge attached to it. She told me to use it to keep Joclyn's lips moist. Joclyn was completely dehydrated. She was not allowed to drink. Drinking liquid with a breathing tube can lead to choking. Each time I held the wet sponge on her lips to moisten them, Joclyn used her tongue to pull the sponge into her mouth hoping for the smallest drop of water. I disobeyed the nurses' orders and kept soaking the sponge for her, desperately trying to help satisfy her insatiable thirst. Luckily, she did not choke.

Eventually, the nurse and physician's assistant came in to see if Joclyn could breathe significantly on her own to have the breathing tube removed. They held this tube to her mouth and told her to breathe in as hard as she could. Joclyn gave a weak effort. The numbers were low. The physician's assistant told us she would have to come back later. In hospital talk, later means four to five hours if you are lucky.

The thought of Joclyn having to go on for that long of a time with the tube in her throat terrified both of us. Joclyn was upset but very tired. I decided she required some motivation. At that moment I put my face up to hers and whispered "Do you really want this breathing tube in your throat for the rest of the day? They are going to give you another shot at this. You are going to give everything you've got and suck in every ounce of oxygen in this room. Then you can drink all you want." Joclyn nodded with what looked like enthusiasm. I ran to pull the physician's assistant and nurse back into the room for another try.

As they prepared Joclyn for her second attempt, I continued to pump her up with inspiring comments. Mostly, I stuck with reminding her how good it was going to feel to gulp down a bottle of cold Peach Snapple Iced Tea. Her eyes bulged out of her head as her way of communicating she was pumped up and ready to suck in oxygen.

Motivated by the thought of unlimited Snapple Iced Tea, as well as a natural desire to get this thick plastic tube out of her throat, Joclyn passed the test on her second attempt. A few minutes later it was out, and Joclyn was back to breathing on her own. I asked her how it felt and she tried to answer me but nothing came out of her mouth. It is funny how many times Joclyn and I have said, "It is amazing how many things can happen to [her or me] that would be considered a horrible thing in someone else's life, but is just another inconvenience in our life." News that came our way was that Joclyn's vocal cord was scratched, and that it would probably be six months until she could speak normally again. For the moment, Joclyn could not make a sound. Shaking her head "yes" and "no," and writing in the journal that Charlene had brought her earlier in the week, would now be her only way to communicate.

I was more concerned about the internal bleeding. I hoped to get through the next day without improperly functioning surgical drains. I was not sure I could handle the idea of her going back into the operating room because of more bleeding. Joclyn was annoyed with her new disability. She had been basically comatose for the past 36 hours, and she had lots she wanted to say. So began her communication via ink and paper. The first thing she wrote was "Iced Tea!!!" I was told to give her liquid slowly as her breathing recovered. This was no easy task. Joclyn sucked down every drop of liquid I put within range. We went back and forth between iced tea and water. Eventually, after she had consumed about a half-gallon of mixed fluids, Joclyn was satisfied. It was time to deal with the reality of where we stood following the operation, and what would come next.

Joclyn had no doubt noticed that of the four tubes with which she entered this most recent surgery, two remained. She also noticed the little LVAD unit at her side pumping the left side of her heart. Before I could explain what had happened and what I was told would happen next, Joclyn wrote something that made my stomach turn. It made me grab her as firmly as a person in her condition could tolerate. I did not let go. I realized what she remembered about the past 12 hours when she wrote, "I thought I was going to die. The nurse kept yelling she was trying to save me and asking if I wanted to die." I assured her it was fine and the doctors had everything under control. I did not tell her that for a while I too thought she was going to die. The next thing Joclyn wrote assured me that she knew I was by her side before the surgery. She remembered me telling her everything was going to be okay. I was glad I made it to the hospital before she went into surgery.

Joclyn

Anesthesia during surgery decreases the body's ability to breathe on its own, and so for this reason a breathing tube, or endotracheal tube, is inserted to assist. It is removed when the person can breathe well on his or her own. Being intubated happened (at least for me) once under anesthesia, but the tube removal, extubation, occurred when somewhat awake. Luckily, while I was intubated and extubated four times in all, I only have the vaguest memory of the last one, and only one traumatic memory from the first time. (Not counting losing my voice from having my vocal cords nicked after the second intubation/extubation, which was an affliction all to itself.)

Following the first surgery, the CentriMag insertion, I think I must have had the tube in for quite some time afterwards. Did I actually write "Am I going to die?" on a pad and hand it to Jeremy? He batted it away and rubbed a sponge lollipop dipped in water (Snapple?) onto my lips. I tried to eat the sponge. I had so many questions. I could only ask as fast as I could write. The tube seemed to block my nose, making writing difficult. This made focusing on the fine motor a job only for my peripheral vision.

A new white coat told me to take a deep breath. She was there to remove the tube, but all of a sudden she was walking away and I was thirsty. Jeremy told me that I wouldn't be able to drink anything for several more hours if I didn't take a deep enough breath. I think I practiced. Jeremy stood up and then the new white coat came back. She counted to three and laughed. I must have done what she wanted. She expertly pulled out the tube — I don't recall gagging — and I was free to breathe and talk like a person again. My first words were surely a complaint or a request of some kind, which no one heard since I had no voice. I don't think I was allowed to drink immediately, though, as those blue sponge lollipops seemed to have stuck around for quite a while.

Weeks later, immediately post-heart transplant, I tried to talk while the tube was still in. No throat vibration or sound is as scary as you could imagine it might be. Happily, I must have fallen asleep because my next memory includes no breathing tube and two nurses standing over me, thrilled when I opened my eyes.

CHAPTER 21

ALL BLEEDING STOPS, EVENTUALLY

Jeremy

So it looked like another few days of waiting around hoping nothing else went wrong until we could get these tubes out of my wife and get her home with some kind of device. At this point we still had hope she could go home by the end of the year. The doctors were hopeful the right side of the heart was improving enough to continue on its own. This would facilitate the removal of the CentriMag device that was assisting the right side of her heart, and leave us with a portable device that would free us to return home until a heart became available. Joclyn was not happy about losing her ability to speak, but the thought of going home had her in great spirits. At this point she had been in the hospital for 13 days, and wanted out. I was starting to wear down as well. I welcomed the sleep and rest that would accompany the return to our home.

The weekend was happily uneventful as far as Joclyn's health went. The drainage tubes were ready to be removed, and they did not show any indication of internal bleeding. Saturday was action-packed with a steady flow of visitors bearing all kinds of gluten-free treats for Joclyn to enjoy. Joclyn's primary challenge was summarizing all that she had to say so that she could write quickly enough to keep up with the conversation in the room. Charlene came on Sunday morning and washed Joclyn's hair. Joclyn was smiling the whole time. It was great to see her so happy. I got to break away for a while and hang out with Mo. We caught up with things that were happening in the world outside the hospital. Apparently, the world keeps moving forward as do the lives of everyone in it. It was great to be brought back in the loop. I shared my excitement at the prospect of bringing Joclyn home to involve her in this as well.

There were also visits from friends that I never would have expected. A longtime friend of mine, John Lennon — not the former Beatle or his ghost, but a coworker from my days in sales in the technology world — told me he wanted to come up from Philadelphia with his wife Maria to visit Joclyn. We had stayed in touch over the past ten years mostly by phone, though we got together when one of us happened to be in the other's city. So I was surprised their visit was purely motivated to see Joclyn. It was great to see them, and we were flattered they had come all the way to Manhattan to visit us. Afterwards, they left to dinner. I recommended "John's Pizza," which had a location only a few blocks away. John had a deep respect for my knowledge and taste in good food. He did not hesitate to head right over. Joclyn was blown away and appreciated their visit. It meant so much to us to have different people from our lives support us during such a difficult and challenging time.

It was rare to have a couple of quiet days without any incidents. Each time it happened, we would wonder how long it would last. Aside from losing her ability to speak, Joclyn was holding up quite well, considering she had her chest opened up twice in 36 hours. She was just starting to recover from the ordeal when one of the resident doctors told us it was time to remove her swan. This was very good news. The swan is a device that is inserted into an artery in her neck and really restricted her movement to an almost unbearable extent. We welcomed the news.

We were not so glad when its removal led to an explosion of blood that splattered all over the floor resident's white jacket. They had taken Joclyn off blood thinners. Evidently, those drugs remained effective. The doctor quickly applied pressure to the area, which was very painful for Joclyn. It goes without saying that applying pressure to a site on a human body that recently held a tube would be painful. Every time the doctor removed the gauze pad he was pressing into Joclyn's neck, blood poured from the opening.

I began to get nervous. Apparently, the doctor noticed my nerves, because he assured us that "all bleeding stops." I took little comfort in this reassurance. Sure, I thought, all bleeding stops, but sometimes bleeding stops because there is no more blood in the human body. After about an hour, the bleeding finally did stop. Still, it was another upsetting chapter of pain and discomfort for her. For me, it caused anguish that defies description.

Joclyn

Melissa and Austin picked up our dog Sedaris from the dog daycare place in Brooklyn that first night. She lived with them for my entire ride through the hospital. Melissa also came to visit me in the hospital many, many times. Those visits involved Chinese delivery and the Fables graphic novels. She got me the first three in the series. Having not picked up a comic book since junior high school, probably, I was a little unsure as to whether I would enjoy them. But they really are intriguing.

"I'd almost rather be at work" again flashed into my mind. I wondered if it was ironic that at my first job as an occupational therapist, I ran "cardiac group" and taught people with sternal precautions — the precautions one must follow for a period of time following open-heart surgery (which of course involves cracking open the sternum) so it will heal properly and not separate — how to do things like get out of bed and put their clothing on without pushing or pulling too much or reaching their arms overhead. I used to even joke with the patients that I always got out of bed as though I had sternal precautions so I wouldn't wake Sedaris before I was ready to take her out for walk number one. Maybe that's why I got sick: I taunted the gods by minimizing the importance of specific post-surgical preventative measures.

Also notable is that no one ever told me a lot of important things about how to take care of myself post-open-heart surgery. No one ever mentioned "sternal precautions" even though my chest had been cracked open and my sternum slash breastbone wired shut, putting it in dire need of precautionary treatment. While the sternum is healing, *precautions* must be taken in order to maximize healing, minimize the risk of infection, and create some all-around comfort. I was also on my own about avoiding the process of skin breakdown, bedsores, the necessity of changing positions when sitting or lying down, what to look for to ensure that my skin was fully intact and supple and all of the other healthy skin adjectives, or how to monitor my multitude of healing surgical wounds. Luckily, I came to the situation already knowing these things. Someone left a walker in my room for me to use. Using a walker while acutely post open-heart surgery might create a medical emergency. It's good that I knew what I know. This walker was really short, too, like maybe I was supposed to walk on my knees with it, or perhaps loan it to a passing child with a gait abnormality.

My education also reminded me to shift my weight off of my sacrum, roll onto my side, and not lift my arms up too high. If anyone had asked, I would have refused helping them to move any furniture, even if they'd helped me move in the past, and I did not allow anyone to grab my hands if trying to help me up. No one had told me that. I imagined that I was not the patient, but rather the therapist sent in to educate me. I would have brought in a diagram that showed skin in the various stages of breakdown — even though it seemed like an unnecessary, fearsome burden to foist upon a patient who was already dealing with a life-shattering illness or injury. That way, patients could see what could happen if they were not diligent and proactive about their own health and safety. I would have shown them these pictures, and I would have told them exactly what measures to take so as to avoid what they depict. No amount of precaution is a guarantee, I would have to also explain. But certainly in the case of a person who has normal sensation, and can tell when they've been in the same position for too long, regular repositioning should help them avoid painful and slow-healing bedsores. I would suggest that they overcompensate for their current state of limited mobility by shifting their weight every 15 minutes while sitting, and to turn their bodies every two hours while sleeping. I'd laugh with them while discussing how one might change position while asleep. I'd put up a sign for the nurses. We'd also laugh and place over/under bets on how many times that sign would be ignored.

No one did that for me, and I'm pretty sure that I would have developed at least a Stage 2 wound if I hadn't already known. When all was said and done I had lost an entire 41 pounds while in the hospital, 139 to 98, and nothing likes to damage skin quite as insidiously as one's own bony prominences. My sacrum ached and all I did was shift around. So lucky for me. At least one nurse said, "We'll need to keep an eye on that," while rolling me around in bed one evening.

Following the internal bleeding extra surgery ultra-emergency, an escalation from our standard state of emergency, I was temporarily taken off of all blood-thinning medication. A day or two after that, my clinical team decided to remove the swan catheter from my neck. Unfortunately, apparently, blood thinners have a longer-than-understood half-life and stick around, working their blood thinning, non-clot forming magic for quite some time. Normally when a catheter is removed, pressure is applied to the site for a brief time and then it can be covered with some gauze and rechecked from time to time to make sure that proper clotting has occurred. When my catheter was removed, simply, certainly, because it was mine, blood pulsed and spattered onto the lab coat of the luckiest resident of the day. The pressure this man applied was tortuous. It was just brutal; it felt like he was going to press right through my neck and pinch all of the nerves in my shoulder — it MUST have been too hard, except that it wasn't. Because every time he needed a break (it went on so long that this was done in rotation), the spurty bleeding resumed as uninterrupted as when the catheter was initially removed. His relief was my favorite little nurse who did not press as hard. While her light touch was to my own relief, she was not nearly as effective. She also needed breaks, and so there went my relief as well. I imagine that it stopped eventually, obviously. I think it took an hour. "All bleeding stops," we were told. I was sure mine would stop when I was dead.

CHAPTER 22

HOW SHOCKING

Jeremy

The next day, our lives returned to a relatively normal state. I went to work with the plan of heading to the hospital as soon as I could get out of the building, get home, and make Joclyn a sandwich. It was about 11:00 a.m. when I got the text on my phone that reminded me that "normal" was no longer in our vocabulary. "Honey, my heart rate is way too fast and they are going to have to shock my heart!" As I tried to catch my breath, my cell phone began to vibrate. "Hello?" Suddenly I was talking to a doctor with a heavy Swedish accent whom I had never met before. He explained that he was on Dr. Horn's team and had just returned from a long break. Joclyn's heart rate was at about 160, and they were quite concerned. They decided to perform a procedure that basically entailed shocking Joclyn's heart in order to create the equivalent of a reset. The procedure would take place at about 5:00 p.m. and Joclyn would be put under during it. If I was going to make it to the hospital before Joclyn went under for this procedure, I was going to have to rush over directly from work.

The rest of the workday crawled by. I considered leaving work early. The doctor insisted it was not a big deal and I should just wait until after work. The bigger concern and mystery was why her heart was acting like she was out running at the park. The Cytoxan she was taking was a form of chemotherapy, and was supposed to be keeping the giant cell at bay, in fact test results a few days before that showed it was. I began to realize that the plan for surgery the next day to remove the final CentriMag was slipping away. When I got out of work, I drove straight into the city towards the hospital. I put the car in the usual parking lot and headed up to Joclyn's room. Even with horrendous traffic, I managed to make it there by 4:30. As I ran up and neared her room, I noticed the curtain in her room was closed, which was a common occurrence whenever the nurses were changing bandages or helping Joclyn with going to the bathroom. I turned to the nurses' station and looked at the monitors that show all of the vital signs of the patients. I found my wife's reading and was astonished to see it go from 160 to zero, and then to 60 right in front of my eyes.

I hoped that Joclyn was not too upset when they started the procedure early, before I had arrived. Only another minute passed before the doctor opened up a curtain, and I was able to enter. I found the nurse waking Joclyn up. Joclyn opened her eyes and smiled when she saw me there. She grabbed her pad and wrote, "You made it, I am so nervous about this and can't believe they are going to shock my heart." I smiled as I told her it was already done, and that I had arrived just in time to see it on the monitor. I left out the part where I saw the monitor jump to zero before resetting at 60. No reason to scare her about something else. The doctor had to confirm what I told her; she did not believe it had happened already. From her perspective, she had closed her eyes for a few seconds. Apparently the procedure had worked for the time being. Yet again, this procedure was nothing in Joclyn's new reality. Had someone told me my heart needed shocking to get it working properly, I would have been inconsolable.

Later that evening things got a little hairy. Joclyn's heartbeat was completely unpredictable. At times it would drop to about 20 beats per minute, and then bounce up to 65 beats per minute. Meanwhile, these rapid fluctuations did not affect Joclyn at all. She said she felt fine. I was in a complete panic. I was trying not to throw up. One of the nurses appeared equally as panicked and called the doctor back into the room. Our new friend from Sweden (at least that is my guess) laughed it off and told us everything was fine. I thought "Really? Because my wife's heartbeat keeps dropping down to 20!" Neshama defied her recent Dr. Gloom-and-Doom nickname and assured us the pace of Joclyn's heart was insignificant. She pointed to the LVAD and the CentriMag and insisted that it was the machines that were serving as Joclyn's heart. She reminded us that we should worry about them, if we were going to worry about anything. The LVAD was Neshama's specialty. She clearly took a lot of pride in the device, almost as if it were her child. God forbid there would be anything other than these devices keeping Joclyn alive.

Joclyn

I was told to count backwards from ten seemingly more often than a frequent driver through DUI checkpoints. Besides my standing fear of awakening during a surgical procedure and being unable to alert anyone to the fact that I am no longer anesthetized, my scariest time performing this task was when I counted backwards from ten on the occasion of extreme tachycardia. Again, I didn't really understand why it mattered what my dying heart was doing, since the CentriMag and LVAD were circulating my blood. But my heart rate of 150 or 160, despite the plethora of heart rate retarding drugs I was taking, very much bothered the team working on me. They wanted to shock my heart back into a normal rhythm.

"With paddles? Are you fucking kidding me? I feel fine!"

A doctor, from whom I would later receive a $3,700 bill, gently reminded me that I had been wearing paddles for the entire time I'd been in the hospital so far, that these were sticky stick-on paddles, and that I would be sedated for this event. I pleaded for a delay so that Jeremy could arrive from work. I'd begun to realize that without Jeremy, I'd be dead. How can someone be expected to deal with such monstrously frightening events otherwise?

The anesthesiologist assured me that I would receive Propofol and would not feel a thing. I immediately recognized this as the drug that killed Michael Jackson. The pop star had referred to this drug, I'd heard, as his "milk." Michael Jackson used a powerful, surgical-grade anesthetic as his casual sleep aid. Did that doctor lose his license? I laughed when I saw the Propofol in the IV. It looked like milk.

I may have gotten all the way down to eight. I opened my eyes and Jeremy was standing over me. "When are they going to do it? I'm really terrified." Jeremy laughed, albeit nervously. They had just done it. Jeremy said he'd been running full speed through the hallways, stopped at the nurses' desk before getting to my room, and saw one of the heart monitors — mine, apparently — instantly change from 160 to 60. He'd guessed they'd done it. I'd guessed they had as well.

CHAPTER 23

STATUS 1A

Jeremy

The next day I was back at work. I thought about how crazy it was that I felt happy and excited about spending my holiday vacation in the hospital. Working and always worrying about what was happening with Joclyn was exhausting. Her voice was coming back as a rough whisper, but not nearly strong enough for her to talk on the phone. Vacation was only a couple of days away. I would be able to spend 11 days by her side without any distractions. I hoped she would come home before the end of the holiday break, but I was unsure, given the events of the day before. It was about 2:00 p.m. as my workday was nearing an end, that I received a phone call as I was watching the students enjoy their class holiday party. "Hello?" I waited nervously for a response, as I was well aware by the caller ID that it was the hospital calling. "Mr. Krevat, this is the physician's assistant; we are attempting to put your wife on the priority list for a transplant. If we are successful she could get a new heart at any moment."

I do not think my feelings had ever been so conflicted about anything in my entire life. Joclyn's heart was in such bad shape that she needed to be moved to the top of the transplant list. This meant she was not going home. She was going to stay right there until a heart arrived. On the other hand, the thought of going home and taking responsibility for the device that kept my wife alive caused me to lose sleep. We did not know how long it would take for the heart to become available. We could have lived in limbo for a year, or even longer. With this news, the possibility that I might spend a year maintaining the machines that replaced Joclyn's heart, and providing her with nursing care, evaporated. Joclyn's priority position on the transplant list served as a stark reminder to us just how sick she was; it was also a glimmer of light at the end of the tunnel. The promise of a new heart meant going home permanently two or three weeks after the transplant. If Joclyn was approved, we were three weeks from being home at any moment: three weeks away from getting our life back.

By the time I got to the hospital the news of Joclyn's approval had arrived. Apparently having an extremely rare disease that is eating away at your heart is enough to get you on top of the list, especially when you are 32 years old. The staff at the hospital was celebrating all of this as great news. I realized that I had no reason to feel conflicted; this was all very good news indeed. Joclyn was in high spirits as well. I found her in a very good mood, and she mouthed the words "Home soon" as I entered the room. The only thing left was to wait and hope. Another positive from all this was the end of my training with Neshama. There was no longer any need for me to learn how to change a bandage while keeping it sterile. I did not have to worry about what to do if the LVAD alarm went off while we were in the living room, watching the Superbowl. Until a heart came, this would be the responsibility of the trained nursing staff.

One thing that hung over our heads, and disturbed us, was Joclyn's heart monitor jumping from 10 to 50. There's nothing like a heart rate of ten to inspire confidence and brighten the mood.

Fortunately, her heart rate was not really that important. As long as the machines were up and running, blood pumped throughout her body. I was just uncertain about what would happen if her heart completely stopped. I was afraid to ask, so I just let the fear dwindle in the back of my mind. I sat down next to the physician's assistant and we talked about the expected waiting time for a new heart. I comforted myself with the memory that Joclyn had a common blood type, increasing the probability of finding a heart sooner, rather than later.

As we sat there that night, Christmas Eve only a couple of days away, we talked about how 15 days was a good guesstimate of how long it would take for the phone to ring with news of a heart. The sense that it could happen at any moment brought a feeling of excitement and anxiety that married to form a tense energy. This tension increased when we were given pamphlets containing information and statistics about heart transplants. I felt a sick twist in my stomach as I read the 5% fatality rate, and the increased likelihood of developing diabetes and/or cancer for transplant recipients.

We also knew we had to beware the false alarm. When waiting for a heart transplant, it is not uncommon to get the call, only to find out it is a false alarm. Here is how I explained it on CaringBridge to all of our friends and family:

> Just to prepare you all. It is very common for false alarms when it comes to getting a heart for these reasons:
>
> 1. They do a blood swap to make sure the compatibility is optimal, if not, she comes back here to NY Pres.
>
> 2. Sometimes a heart looks good on paper, but when the team at Columbia looks at it, they reject it.
>
> It is not uncommon for her to make 1–2 trips that end up with her coming back.
>
> But this is all due to how picky and selective the team at Columbia is, they are going to make sure she gets a good strong heart.

Joclyn

I was thereafter assured that this had been a very good thing. Because of this episode of heart rate fluctuation, I was to be bumped up on the heart waiting list to "1A" status. 1A is the highest priority. People who are on the 1A list are in an ICU and will die soon without a transplanted organ. 1B... oh, for the fullest, most horrifying effect, I'll just copy and paste the definitions from my scary memory-refreshing Google search.

Status 1A

Patients who must stay in the hospital and require IV drugs, a heart assist device, a ventilator, or who have a life expectancy of a week or less without a transplant. If you are under 18 years of age, you may be Status 1A with slightly less severe problems. Status 1A patients have the highest priority on the waiting list

Status 1B

Patients who are not confined to the hospital, but who require a heart assist device or continuous IV meds while at home (or wherever). Some of the newer assist devices do allow a patient to wait at home. Status 1B patients have the second-highest priority on the waiting list

Status 2

All other "active" patients on the transplant waiting list. If you are a Status 2 patient waiting at home, you will be seen at regular intervals by your transplant cardiologist, probably once every 4 weeks. You will have a right heart cath about every 3 months to check your pulmonary pressures. While you wait, remember to be prepared!

Status 7

Patients who are temporarily inactive, meaning they are not waiting to get that call right now for some reason

Relative, but good, apparently. If a matching heart became available anywhere within a 4–5 hour flight, it would be mine. I was excited by this news, but also became very sad for all of the people who have Type O blood who had been waiting much longer than I. What unlucky bastards they are. Also relative.

CHAPTER 24

A MISSED FLIGHT

Jeremy

A couple of days passed, and Christmas arrived. We were supposed to be on a plane to San Diego to visit my brother Lee and his family. Joclyn and I were depressed about being in the hospital instead. The good news was that vacation had began, and I was able to spend entire days with Joclyn, without her having to wait for me to finish work. It was great to be with her during the day, and not have to look at the clock constantly. With all this free time we decided to finally stop talking about it, and went on to Netflix to watch season one of *Dexter*. We had a lot of time to kill and we had heard great things about this show. We figured getting into a new series would distract us from the constant thought of hearts and transplants. Joclyn and I watched the first episode. We were both immediately hooked. We loved the show. We must have torn through three episodes before coming up for air.

For those few hours it seemed like our lives were back to normal. It was just my wife and I watching television without a care in the world — at least until the nurse came in for the shift change and threw me out of the room to do the changeover procedures. It was back to the waiting room for me. When the nurses had a shift change, the new nurse had to run a whole checklist of annoying things like confirming Joclyn had no pulse, and check that she was still breathing regardless. I was always kicked out of the room, and I took my usual spot in the waiting room.

While in the waiting room I got a reminder of what it was like to be in the cardiac unit of a hospital. A young woman in her early twenties was sitting across from me with her mother. The woman cried as she tried to explain to her mother that her husband was very sick: "Dad is dying, Mom, he is not waking up." I sat there with several other people in the waiting room with my face down, looking at the floor wishing there was something I could do. As bad as things were for Joclyn and me, I was constantly reminded of just how much worse things could get. A few days later, a woman was crying to her brother to call and have the flowers delivered. I went over and gently informed her to save her money, because they do not allow flowers in the ICU, but she explained that they were for the funeral. Her father was dying and only had a few hours left. I felt horrible and offered my condolences. I would not suggest hanging out in an ICU waiting room as a leisurely activity.

So the wait through the holidays continued and we tried not to think about the obvious statistic that proves more people drive drunk and get into car accidents around the holidays and on New Year's Eve. It is a horrible dilemma to hope for a new heart, because you are in fact hoping someone has a fatal brain crushing death in order to provide a heart for the person you love. To deal with this dilemma and the guilt that comes along with it, we told ourselves that accidents are going to happen. We just hoped the victims were kind enough to become organ donors, because they hoped their death could help others. We had no choice but to convince ourselves we were honoring that person's wishes, and committed ourselves to cherishing their generosity and taking great care of the heart they left for us.

Joclyn

So back to *Dexter*. I so looked so forward each evening to watching this show with Jeremy. His visits were the highlight of each day, and his were the most regular. I might even say that our *Dexter* viewings were the highlight of the highlight. The best days were when we would watch two episodes. That would create a two-hour space in time where we could become totally absorbed (save the multiple nursing interruptions) in the life of Miami Metro Police Department blood spatter analyst Dexter Morgan. I think it helped that we watched the show on my laptop and had headphones in our ears. Maybe the headphones made us feel safe and insulated, or maybe it was just that watching television for a couple of hours in the evening was something that real people did, like the kinds of people who didn't have to stay in hospitals until someone tragically, yet organ-preservedly died and had previously decided to give a most benevolent death gift. Of course, I think that we both enjoyed talking to each other. I cherished Jeremy's retelling of his Real World Experiences, those in which he sleeps in an apartment in Brooklyn, goes to work, and then also goes to graduate school in the evenings. He didn't have to tell me that then he'd also go visit his wife (of six months) who was waiting in a cardiac ICU for a heart transplant, because that's the part I got to know about without anyone telling me. The problem with talking to each other was that we were both so anxiously traumatized, and we would eventually circle back to talking about being in the hospital and needing and waiting for a heart transplant, and no one should ever talk about that.

CHAPTER 25

NEW YEAR'S DOWN THE SHORE

Jeremy

Our families continued to visit. Matthew and Madhavi were in town for the holidays. While Madhavi stayed with Joclyn in the hospital, Matthew and I took the opportunity to get out. I remembered that there was that John's Pizza I had recommended to John Lennon, and assumed it was the same or close to the original one on Bleecker Street. It's funny the things I chose to worry about, because when I discovered the pizza at this location was not nearly as good, I remember worrying that I had given my friend a bad recommendation and wasted his opportunity to experience great New York City pizza. My brother brought me back to the moment when he suggested another round of beers, which never disappoint. These breaks from the hospital did not come often. I tried to keep my mind off Joclyn so I could recharge.

New Year's Eve came: we spent the evening watching reruns of *Jersey Shore*. I justify this choice by arguing that it beats watching *Dick Clark's New Year's Rockin' Eve with Ryan Seacrest*. As we got closer to New Year's Eve, we turned on Dick Clark's show. The show featured only a few minutes of Dick Clark. The stars of *Jersey Shore* were guest hosts on this channel as well. Joclyn laughed, which I always appreciated, and we watched the ball drop, signaling an end to the biggest roller coaster of a year I could have ever dreamed of. As we all celebrated the beginning of a new year, Joclyn started to cry. She did not have to explain. I took her hand and made her a promise. "Next year we will not be in a hospital, we will be in a much better place, and this will all be a memory." Joclyn wiped away some tears and I held her as best I could given the tubes going in and out of her chest and arms.

There have been fewer depressing days in my life than January 1st. The worst part of it for me had always been the end of the holidays and the return to normal life, whether that meant school or the workplace. This year it was both wrapped up in one, since I am employed by the New York City Department of Education. If Joclyn had been healthy, this would have been the first year where I felt no such depression. My job change was a complete success; I loved my job and never minded going to work. But going back to work meant leaving Joclyn alone for hours every day. This was horribly depressing for both of us, and the crazy schedule of rising, going to work, rushing to the hospital, and going home to sleep was about to return.

My graduate courses would not begin for the spring semester until the end of January, which was the saving grace of my return to work after the holidays. To celebrate our last day of my vacation, I ran out and got us both some chow fun, naturally gluten-free. We watched a few episodes of *Dexter* and saw an older patient who also had an LVAD device go home. His device was not a bridge to a heart transplant; it was to extend his life for as long as possible. On the way out I hugged his wife, and as I shook his hand, he looked up at me and promised, "She will be all right, and soon you will be going home as well. God bless you." I was happy for them, but sad to see them go. They had been one of the constants in this place, and now they were gone. Things were changing around us, but our situation was the same. That feeling quickly changed when we were told Joclyn would be getting his room the next day. It was the corner room used for patients who were in the hospital for long-term stays. Joclyn was now the senior person in the unit, a position she would have gladly relinquished for a new heart and a trip home.

Joclyn

Having never heard of it before, I also watched *Jersey Shore*, the polar opposite of *Dexter*, during my ICU encampment. It seemed like no matter when I turned on the television, there was Snooki being punched in the face by some guy she'd been fucking with. "This is the worst thing that could possibly happen," she would later lament. "Oh is it?" I would laugh. My good friend Charlene had introduced me to the show, and she too would marvel at how vapid and wrong these Jersey Shore folks were, and how limited their life experiences were. I think I am quite highly qualified, at this point, to speak on the topic of the worst thing that could possibly happen. I wish that the worst thing that had ever happened to me was that I bothered a gorilla juice head (Jersey Shore talk for a reference to someone who takes steroids, which, of course, I do, but I guess I take the wrong kind to fall into favor with the over-thirty vanity crowd) in a bar until he got so fed up with my stupidity that he hit me. Granted, on the occasion of the first time I saw *Jersey Shore*, I had only had three open-heart surgeries to date. I'd subsequently have one more, so maybe I should have held my hate until then. It can always get worse, even for us.

How did my husband handle all of this? For whom was it worse?

It seemed like New Year's Eve was the perfect time to procure an organ. By all accounts, not just my own imagination, lots of perfectly healthy people meet their demise on that night. Roadblocks and spot checks don't stop folks from driving drunk, driving into things, and suffering catastrophically irreversible brain damage, the exact kind of injury that can occur and leave all of the other major organs intact and healthy and suitable for swapping with broken ones — like my heart. My proverbial heart was very much not broken at that moment, funnily enough. I mean, I was infinitely furious with the universe for having done this to me, but my family was there, and without them I may as well have been dead. Alone, staring at the walls of my hospital room would have been torture beyond the cruel joke of which I had become the butt. Also, New Year's Eve might be an occasion for someone on life support to be taken off. People also like to try to off themselves around Christmas time, perhaps after realizing that they cannot satisfy the expectations of their families with gifts or money or whatever success they have not achieved. In the spirit of starting anew, lots of painful decisions might be made on New Year's Eve.

It wasn't meant to be my night, though, and as Matthew, Madhavi, and Jeremy left at 12:30 on January 1st, I was pretty certain that it would be a very long time before the good news came.

CHAPTER 26

BUSINESS CLASS

Jeremy

The new room was great. It was three times the size of Joclyn's previous room, had a cot for me to spend the night, and a full table with chairs to give the room a more homey feel. Since the room was larger, it was better suited to accommodate the growing pile of our possessions. When word got out that Trader Joe's offered lots of Joclyn's favorite gluten-free treats, bags of snacks arrived every week with our visitors. Stan and Eileen, Mo's parents, and my childhood neighbors, showed up with four packages of beef jerky, and two full bags of other items from the Trader Joe's next door to them in Edgewater, New Jersey. The new space and generosity of our friends made the place feel a little more like a home, and made us feel very grateful. We were not sure how much longer we would have to wait for a heart. But the previous eight days felt like a lifetime.

Joclyn

Soon after, I was transferred to the bigger room mentioned earlier. This was a momentous event for us, and a great relief. First of all, it had room for a roll-away cot which meant that Jeremy could spend an overnight here and there with me. (Lucky him!) It also had a table, more shelf space, and a spaciously deep windowsill area. I had acquired a lot of snacks and goods. The windowsill, per the Joint Commission (formerly the Joint Commission on Accreditation of Healthcare Organizations), was not an acceptable place to store them. And so every few days, when an inspection was pending, a nurse would frantically shuffle about all of my stuff. This endlessly infuriated Jeremy, who could then never find anything when he arrived by my side following work.

CHAPTER 27

BLOOD-SUCKING VAMPIRES

Jeremy

Things got back to "normal" as we adjusted to my return to work. However, new problems arose to fill our days with gut-wrenching stress. Blood counts were the new scare of the day. Joclyn's counts were down and close to a level that would remove her from the transplant list if they dipped any lower. I was frustrated because it seemed like five different teams of doctors kept taking blood from her throughout the day. Everyone needed her blood for tests. I wondered why they did not share the same sample of blood and run all of the tests. I felt there must be a reason they were all taking the blood separately. At one point she was so close to be taken off the list they gave her a medication that helps her body produce new blood. My stress level rose when Joclyn announced it was a $1,000 charge each time they administered the medication. I wondered if my insurance company would try to deny coverage. Our financial situation was not great with just the salary of a first-year teacher coming in each month.

Every day at about 6:00 p.m. a team of doctors would come in to update us on things and do a routine evaluation. One day in early January, I had finally had enough of the vampires that came in several times to take blood from my wife. To my way of thinking, even a brief disruption to Joclyn's presence on the transplant list represented disaster. Joclyn was losing weight and her feet were beginning to swell. I was wondering how long she could live with machines doing the job of her heart. I could tell from our visitors' faces that Joclyn was looking worse each day. I finally spoke up. "Why are you taking so much of her blood every day? Can't you use one sample for all the tests?" The team looked around at each other and asked what I meant.

I explained that five different teams of doctors were taking blood each day for different tests. I wondered if those teams understood her situation and how costly each drop of blood was to her continued presence on the transplant list. They were quiet for a few seconds and then shocked me by agreeing with me and promising they would look into the matter. They also noted that I raised an interesting point. It was in those few minutes that I realized why every patient in a hospital needs an advocate. The individual teams each had their own agenda, and nobody was communicating with one another. I realized I would have to take on that responsibility. That was the moment I became a true caretaker. I was never afraid to speak up again, and it was not long afterwards that I had to do just that.

Joclyn

This may have been the event that prompted Jeremy to take a stand and be adamant about saying no to doctors when necessary.

Having worked in hospitals, I went into this knowing something that not a lot of other people know about hospitals. Doctors do not have the last word, and they often don't know what the other doctors are up to. They can be wrong. Jeremy was hesitant to adopt my knowledge of How Things Work early on in my medical disaster, but as the days turned into weeks and he witnessed up close how we were sometimes fed conflicting information, he turned into a fabulous patient advocate. An unanswered call bell motivated him to briskly strut down the hall to the nurses' station. Jeremy, seeing my discomfort at being ignored, made sure we were heard and my needs met.

The constant, apparently redundant, blood draws really were what turned everything around for both of us in terms of ever feeling nervous about speaking up regarding quality of care. Any anxiety we felt about being proactive vanished. The immunology team was fascinated by my blood and me. They often came in to draw vials of it for examination. They were especially interested in examining my blood when they suspected that I may have had some type of infection. The concern was that every evening, my body temperature seemed to rise to around 100 degrees. They thought that by examining a large amount of my blood, the cause would be easily determined.

Coinciding with this interest, of course, was a need — as dictated by the heart failure team — to keep my blood counts up so I would be allowed to remain on the transplant list. To me, this was the priority. The reason I could not go home was because I was waiting for a new heart. Waiting for a new heart while being told that if a donor heart became available I would not be allowed to accept it would have been just a brutal turn of events. The heart failure team told me repeatedly that if my counts went any lower than whatever the magic cutoff was, I would convert to a Status 7 on the transplant list and essentially lose my spot in line.

They did not tell this to the immunology people, who insisted on continuing their pattern of drawing blood. This team even announced a plan to take "many vials" of blood to enact certain specialized tests.

Jeremy, on my behalf, put a stop to this insistence by telling them, forcibly, what the transplant team had told us. After some refusal and penis waving, at least one of the doctors told us that we were right, and this battle was won. I was allowed to keep my blood. The multi-headed monster does not talk to itself. Reason number one million that I cannot imagine how anyone can survive as an inpatient without a spouse or other medical advocate getting things done.

Feeling imprisoned choked me. I think I must have lived hour to hour while waiting for the heart, like a recovering alcoholic who can only imagine TODAY without a drink, but on a microcosmic level. "Since it is 2:00 now, I am certain that I will survive until 3:00." The gown choked me. Even if it was tied loosely, it made me touch my neck and force a swallow nervously. The endless requests of my body choked me. The occasional X-ray technician who forgot to put the lead vest on me before leaving the room for his own safety drove me to hate. I don't know why I rarely said something. When I did, they were always about to cover me up anyway. I still cared what people thought about me, and I still always touch my neck sometimes and swallow nervously.

CHAPTER 28

JUST PRAY?

Jeremy

The nurses at Weill Cornell are outstanding. They kept us going each day and I do not know how I would have survived the stress of not being with Joclyn while I was at work. They take excellent care of their patients. Joclyn would always text me and let me know who took over each shift, and I would feel such great relief when it was Arvin, Jojo, or Derrick, etc. I always felt anxious when I heard a new name because I was afraid they might not be as attentive and caring as the nurses we had grown to trust. One evening as I was preparing to go home the nurse for the evening entered the room and introduced herself. I recognized her voice right away as the nurse I spoke to on the phone when she called me to tell me that Joclyn was bleeding internally. I had a bad feeling about her and the way she spoke to me that morning, but remembered that she was probably under a lot of stress when she made the call. I decided that under normal circumstances she was probably as good as the rest of the staff. I convinced myself of this and left without saying anything to Joclyn.

About an hour later, when I got home to our apartment in Brooklyn, I got a text from Joclyn that the nurse was horrible and saying awful things to her. I felt blood rushing to my head as I considered heading back to the hospital for a war. But I thought better of it as I may have only made the problem worse. It turned out that the nurse scolded Joclyn for requiring assistance returning to bed from her chair. The nurse seemed to think being attached to pumps and a giant machine with tubes coming out of her heart was no excuse to be struggling with mobility. This nurse failed to consider the effects being stuck with barely any way to move around has on the muscles. It had been about a month since Joclyn had walked, not to mention having undergone three open-heart surgeries in the previous four weeks.

The nurse also told Joclyn not to get her hopes up for a heart anytime soon. She estimated it would be a year before she got a new heart. Now this completely contradicted what the doctors and physician's assistants had been telling us for the prior ten days. I promised Joclyn I would take action and not let this nurse get away with this behavior. I was shocked because Brian, the director in charge of all the nurses, was an awesome guy completely on top of everything, and his staff had reflected that since we arrived on their unit. The next day I called Brian to tell him what happened. Brian was quick to reassure me that this nurse was ignorant about how long it would take to find a heart for Joclyn. Brian added that this nurse had no idea that Joclyn was on top of the recipient list. He made it clear it was not her place to say anything either way.

He was shocked she criticized Joclyn for her inability to get in and out of the bed. And, he stressed that it was ludicrous to expect normal mobility from someone in Joclyn's condition. When I spoke to Brian I pointed out that I had never complained once in all the time we were in the hospital. He quickly agreed and told me the entire staff adored us, and he knew my concern and anger was completely valid. He assured me Joclyn would not be assigned this nurse again, and that he was going in to the hospital, even though it was his day off, to have a special meeting with this nurse. True to his word, Brian made sure this nurse did not come anywhere near us again.

Joclyn was amazed about what I had done. I am usually not the confrontational type. Now I was complaining about nurses, making demands, and proving to be a strong advocate on her behalf. I felt like I was growing up in that hospital, and the playful child in me was dying off. I was willing to accept that if it meant being stronger for Joclyn and helping her get through this ordeal. I was always proud of the fact that I refused to let the child in me fade away. I always maintained my sense of humor, and insisted that there was nothing wrong with goofing around and being silly. I was almost 40, but felt like the same person I was as a teenager. Now I felt that slipping away. I was getting angry and scared. Nothing seemed funny anymore. I did not believe the person who came into the hospital with Joclyn existed anymore. I felt different.

Joclyn

The nurse who had, infamously, told me to shut up while I was bleeding internally, advised me one terrible night that I could wait as long as a year for a heart, and that I really ought to be doing more for myself, considering I am so young, and a runner as well. My feet were swollen and felt like the heaviest parts of my body. I needed help to move them in and out of the bed. She did not feel she should have had to help me. I make a fantastic patient, snarky thoughts aside. So, when I texted Jeremy in a nauseated panic, essentially in an enormous state of fear since I quickly realized that I was completely at the mercy of this woman, because I was hooked up to tubes and all, Jeremy called and complained to the social worker and the director of nursing. My concerns were taken quite seriously. Last I heard, this horrid nurse who told me to "just pray" was transferred to a different department, and ultimately terminated from the hospital entirely. The stockroom would be appropriate. Seriously. Why work in a hospital if you hate people? Plenty of professions offer isolation from the general public.

After complaining, I didn't feel any better, either. I feared that she would come into my room while I was asleep and unplug one of the pumps. How could I stop her, were that her whim? She was the one who got to go home after each shift and forget about LVADs and CentriMags and bedpans. She was free to invent horrible things to say to people. I was tethered, not free.

CHAPTER 29

ON AGAIN, OFF AGAIN

Jeremy

On January 7th, I remember thinking we had five more days until we hit the three-week mark on the transplant list. In my mind, waiting three weeks was supposed to be the worst-case scenario, since Joclyn was first on the donor list for the entire east coast region. I started to think a new heart was the answer to all of our problems. Her own heart was barely functioning, and riddled with this unexplainable disease. We continued to face the problems of Joclyn's general state of health; we worried that one of the different teams treating her would diagnose something that required her temporary removal from the transplant list. Still, the teams rarely spoke to one another. There was the team that dealt with the disease itself. There was the team that focused on the heart. There was a general team of the regular residents.

Joclyn's temperature also threatened her position on the transplant list. A fever indicated possible infection, and *any* infection was not desirable for a transplant. The frequency with which the nursing staff took Joclyn's temperature complicated, and clouded this issue. Joclyn ran a normal temperature in the morning, and for most of the day. However, at about 6:00 p.m. she always spiked a slight fever, about 99 degrees. This would lead to an upsetting discussion about a possible infection. I would find myself arguing that we experience this every day. The nursing staff and I resolved to wait until 10:00 p.m. each evening to determine whether or not Joclyn's temperature should concern us. And every night at 10:00 p.m. her temperature would recede to 98.6.

These threats to Joclyn's status on the recipient list began to take a toll on me. I was becoming extremely stressed and irritable. The chemo treatments Joclyn was receiving every ten days were making her sick. I was uncertain why she needed them if her heart was already damaged beyond repair. If she was already dependent on machines to pump her heart, why did they need to continue fighting the disease? When I asked, a doctor explained that it would help reduce the chance the disease would return after she received a new heart. I hated how the chemo affected Joclyn. It made her nauseous, queasy, and extremely tired. The reaction to the chemo usually lasted two to three days, and we could not always plan the visitor schedule around these treatments. Sometimes, especially after a chemo treatment, visitors saw Joclyn at her worst as she waited in the hospital for a new heart.

Joclyn

I was moved to Status 7 on a couple of occasions, however. That was just ridiculous when that happened. Remember, I was trapped in the hospital because I needed a heart transplant, but should a match have become available, I would not have been permitted to accept it as a person with a status of 7. Hearts are not that easy to come by, for your information, in case you hadn't thought about it. Kidneys and livers and bone marrow are easier to procure, as one needn't cease to live to qualify as a donor. One time I was demoted to Status 7 because I'd received a blood transfusion. Oh, that. Yet again an example of what might be the most horrific thing ever to occur in a young, healthy person's life. For me, it was just something that happened that day. I jest, a bit. It was actually a huge deal, and was a prelude to open-heart surgery number 2 (the first being CentriMag placement). I was bleeding internally following that first emergency surgery, and awoke in my room to a crowd. I remember nurses, bags of blood, and that one terrible nurse telling me to shut up because I kept asking for water and asking me if I wanted to die. I heard someone say that Jeremy was coming. I later learned that in those moments, Jeremy had been speeding up to the hospital and cutting off taxis, after having been at work for a full eleven minutes when he received a call telling him to hurry. Hurry, because the team was working to save my life.

Have you ever received such a call while at work? Ever?

I was considered to be on the list but not on the list a second time when my "counts" were low. I'm no chemist, obviously, I mean, I had to take Chem 1 as a prerequisite course to Bio 1 which was a prerequisite to anatomy and physiology which were required for admittance into occupational therapy school. But I don't really know what "your counts are low, therefore you are off the list for a heart but you can't leave because you need a heart" means, exactly, except that it made me very, very angry. Making me angrier still was that once my "counts" were "back up" and I was again a holder of 1A status, the whole vampire fiasco with doctors from every "service" wanting seemingly all of my blood happened. Donating a large amount of blood for this purpose, however, could bring down my "counts," and possibly necessitate a transfusion which would take me off the list. Crying is sometimes disarming, I learned. I won that battle; in fact, the night that the heart arrived, my temperature was 99.5. The nurse assured me that that did not count as a fever. I am glad that what felt like a lie did not come back to bite me in the ass.

CHAPTER 30

CHEMO BRAIN

Jeremy

We really felt for one of our visitors one Saturday. Kyle was the son of Marc's girlfriend Cheryl. At the time he was just about 20 years old, and Kyle clearly had never seen anyone this sick in his life. Joclyn was barely able to keep her eyes open. The chemotherapy exhausted her. For a few days, after chemotherapy treatment, Joclyn's appearance shocked people who didn't know what to expect. Most of the time, an alert, upbeat and youthful Joclyn would greet visitors; they would never guess that disease had destroyed her heart, and that she relied on machines to keep her alive. Kyle did not get to see that Joclyn; he saw a person weakened by chemotherapy. The spark that makes her such a lively person dimmed. It was at these moments that she would actually appear as sick as you would envision when told of her condition. He kept his distance and was very quiet. It was possible he was just not chatty because he does not know us very well, but probably not. I tried to explain the reason for her appearance, but it was impossible to erase the impression Kyle received.

The next day, Joclyn felt bad about the impression she left on Kyle. I told her not to worry. All of our family and friends, including Kyle, would feel better about her state of health when she got her new heart. The arrival of a new heart was going to resolve so much for both of us; it was always on our mind. Joclyn's very existence was about staying alive until that heart came. Not only staying alive, but remaining active on the heart recipient list. Every little thing that could temporarily remove her from that list was our enemy.

We insisted that people sanitize their hands when entering the room. We asked people to keep their distance in case they were contagious. We were obsessed with keeping her as safe from infection as possible. We worried about how long she could continue like this. That new heart was the light at the end of the tunnel. We wondered when it would come.

Joclyn

One Cytoxan infusion hit me harder than the others, and Day 1 post chemo coincided with a visit from my father's girlfriend Cheryl and her son Kyle. Kyle, I later learned, was incredibly worried about me and frequently asked about how I was doing, showing visible relief when the news was good. The day he visited did not assure him of my prospects. I slept for the entire visit, and he was there for hours. He never came that close to me (I was in the large room at this point) and I vaguely remember him weakly smiling when I told him that really, I was okay, but just really, really tired.

I was so tired that I couldn't even lift my head from the pillow.

Jeremy and I felt terrible about this the following day when I was back to (relatively) normal, appetite and all. We wished Kyle could come back and see me in a better state.

Unless it came at the expense of time with Jeremy, Mo, and Charlene, or an out-of-towner, aside from being told I could go home, I had nothing to look forward to but visitors. As most of my friends have jobs, though, I preferred that my mother and her husband, who does not work every day and who is retired, respectively, came during the week so that the weekends could be reserved for people who legitimately could not come on a different day.

My friend Jeff visited, but I was asleep for most of the time he was in my room. He's a bit of a hypochondriac and came pretty much nowhere near me. He did wave and smile at me a few times when there were natural breaks in his conversation with Jeremy, about five feet from the foot of my bed.

CHAPTER 31

KARAWHATKE?

Jeremy

Another unforgettable visit came from Mara and Barry. Mara is a close friend who is very close to my parents, and has become part of our extended family. Barry is a singer-songwriter my family has known for years. My father has performed on stage with both of them, and recorded and produced CDs of their music as well. Joclyn had met Mara a few times and was thrilled when she sang at our wedding. Joclyn was not as familiar with Barry and was surprised she would take the time to visit her. We strongly appreciated their thoughtfulness in visiting Joclyn.

Mara came with a Karaoke machine and was planning on putting on a show for Joclyn. I thought it was humorous that she wanted to do this for us in light of where we were. Mara loves music and understands its healing effects. While we explained that we were in an intensive care unit and this performance might not go over well with the staff, to this day we both kind of wish we hadn't stopped her. She understood and stayed quietly by Joclyn's side with Barry. Looking back, it amazes me how much my parents' friends love them. Mara was so intent on taking our minds off the madness of the hospital and our situation that she was ready to sing to us in an ICU. Barry barely knew Joclyn, yet stayed for over an hour. If not for Joclyn wanting to spend time with Charlene who was waiting behind them, they both seemed ready to stay longer. I realized it was best to spread out visitors, so nobody was waiting to spend time with us.

Joclyn

This may have been the event that prompted me to force Jeremy to take a stand and be adamant about certain people needing to call ahead and schedule their visits.

Mara is a good friend and musical compadre of the Krevats, and she even sang for our walk down the aisle at our wedding while Manny backed her up on guitar. She and I share a birthday. I think she is a pretty cool person. She is a jewelry maker. She interestingly also has a bit of a medical history, in some ways making us common to the knowledge of things not being right.

Her visits to the ICU were obviously welcome. She always came bearing snacks from Trader Joe's or Whole Foods to further cover the window ledges and other *verboten* surfaces that would need to be cleared when "the state" came for an inspection.

One day she came to visit with a plan in mind — clearly. She toted a large amplifier on wheels (I am almost certain) and appeared ready to spend the afternoon singing to me — and the rest of the cardiac intensive care unit. I thought that this was great! But remember that I was the healthiest patient (appearance-wise), and that most other patients on my unit were intubated or otherwise out of it and, unfortunately, doing anything loud just wasn't permitted. While that was the end of it, we still crack up over the thought of it whenever talk of my time in the hospital commences. We really must make a Karaoke date with Mara.

That day Mara brought a Krevat friend with her whom I'd never met, and the two of them stayed, generously, for quite a long time, especially considering we were not close. Mo and Charlene were also visiting that day, and their visits were also very important to me. Mo and Charlene eventually, naturally, had to leave. From that day forward, Jeremy and I were very vocal about what was and was not acceptable for a weekend visit, schedule-wise These rules were directed toward my mother and friends who were not very close friends. Jeremy saw how upset I was about not having enough time with each person, and asked via CaringBridge that visitors prearrange times and days rather than just show up. Most people did, but some others did not respect our request. It was a challenge to explain to people, who had only good intentions, why coordination of everyone's time was so paramount to my comfort and coping.

CHAPTER 32

READ IT OUT LOUD WHILE I BITE

YOUR HEAD OFF

Jeremy

A few days later my sister-in-law Kathy came out to visit from California. Joclyn was feeling better and had recovered from the chemo, so the timing was great. It was also a great help to me because leaving Joclyn alone all day while I was at work was becoming even more stressful, if that was possible, as time passed by. I felt good knowing Kathy was with her those days during the week and would stay until I arrived after work.

Kathy had helped lift Joclyn's spirits a couple of weeks before, when she used some of her contacts in the writing world to prompt an email from David Sedaris. Joclyn is a huge fan of David Sedaris, which is obvious when you consider the name of our dog. People wonder, in confusion, whether we named her after David, the writer, or his actress sister Amy, of *Strangers with Candy*. Anyway, I was very happy to get a text message from Joclyn one morning that read, "David Sedaris sent me an email!" I will always appreciate that Kathy helped provide such a great moment for Joclyn when she really needed it.

Joclyn worried she was not being nice enough to Kathy considering she came so far to visit and help out. I asked Kathy and she did not really understand what Joclyn was talking about. Considering Joclyn's condition, it amazed me that she had the strength and presence of mind to feel concern about that sort of thing. I told her not to worry about it, and that people were happy to see her. As she worried about her appearance and her mood, I assured her that visitors who saw her in the flesh were better off than if they imagined her mood and appearance. I was not sure I believed that in the case of some visits, but I kept those thoughts to myself.

So far my parents had made trips up from North Carolina, my brother and his wife had come from North Carolina, and my oldest brother Lee was due to arrive in less than two weeks from California. While Kathy and Lee were dismayed they could not come together, we were happy to spread their visits out for more time Joclyn would have the benefit of some much-needed company. I was grateful to have such a supportive family. They all love Joclyn, and it was never more evident with all of the traveling and time being dedicated to seeing her through this situation.

Joclyn

Kathy, my other sister-in-law, flew in from San Diego and stayed with a friend in the city. She freakin' READ to me. How hard are you crying right now? A grown woman reading to me, another grown woman, because I didn't have the focus to read more than a page at a time myself. I think I was short with her. I was short with everyone, but no one cared. "Do they sell gluten-free food around here?" I may have snapped a "No, of course not." She may have smiled, but also did manage to rustle up some rice and beans and a protein shake.

Kathy is a writer, and thus has writerly connections. As anyone who knows the name of my dog understands, I am an enormous David Sedaris fan. And so she conspired with her agent and Jeremy to somehow contact David Sedaris, tell him my story, and ask him to write to me. It was an early morning ICU haze that at first told me I had been spammed, and a moment of sharper clarity that kept me from immediately deleting the email from "David Sedaris."

But it was really from him!

David Sedaris <dsedaris@xxxxxx.xxx>

Dear Joclyn,

I'm sorry you've had such rotten luck. I had no idea a viral pneumonia could cause so much damage. It all sounds just awful. I, meanwhile, am off to Japan, which is not all it's cracked up to be, you know. Like sometimes I'll buy something, and the person selling it will not bow as low as he ought to. Other times you'll order dinner, and they'll give you too much. After Japan I'm going to Australia and for that I really need sympathy. Currently in Sydney it's 110 degrees and raining mud.

Sincerely,
David Sedaris

I would attend one of his book signings years after receiving his email. He signed a printed copy of it. He laughed when he reread it. And my life was complete.

CHAPTER 33

SUPERSTITIONS

Jeremy

During an extended hospital stay, anything to pass the time is welcome. It is always nice if you can actually find forms of entertainment that make you feel normal. Getting into *Dexter* helped. Luckily Netflix made the first couple of seasons available for streaming. We were also fortunate to have nurses that loved Joclyn. A new doctor came into our room after hearing about our desire to kill more time. He began to set up a DVD player that included a long cable. It hooked into the small television that was mounted in the ceiling. This would be easier than holding the computer between us which had become uncomfortable. He also told us the last patient that used this player got his heart within 48 hours so maybe it was lucky. To this, Joclyn whispered, "I will take all the luck I can get." I had to repeat it for the doctor, as I became the expert on what Joclyn was trying to say whenever she attempted to speak.

After the DVD player was set up, the on-duty nurse came in with the movie *The Hangover*. She informed us of how much all the nurses loved this movie and how funny it is. Joclyn and I remembered the trailers for this film on television before she got sick. Although it had been about six weeks since this whole saga began, it felt like months had passed. The movie was very funny and we both laughed and escaped our reality for a couple of hours. It was nice, and we appreciated what the staff in the hospital was doing for us. I needed the break. I was getting very paranoid by this time. I did not understand how Joclyn could survive any longer with a heart that was all but dead. I could not get a clear answer on how long she could survive on these CentiMag devices. The answer depended on who you asked, and as humans we tend to focus on the lease desirable answer. In this case the answer that haunted me was an on-call resident doctor who simply stated, "We need this heart to come sooner rather than later."

Joclyn

God bless Netflix streaming. First of all, regarding Netflix streaming, I'm not sure what I would have done otherwise, televisionally-speaking. The hospital rooms at both Weill Cornell and Columbia were not equipped with typical hospital room-sized televisions mounted on walls, but rather each bed had a swinging arm on it with a nine-inch television attached to it. The arm didn't reach around enough so as to position the television into the comfortable viewing position I like to call "in front of me." It only reached far enough that it could be seen by turning 45 degrees to the left. It was as if the designer had decided that hospitalized people do not deserve to watch television with company. The patient should be the entertainment for the visitors, and the patient should only watch television when alone, and propped on one elbow, swan-neck catheter in her neck and all.

The discomfort of the television situation went unnoticed by no one. We were gifted with a loan of a DVD player, which — while it did not increase the size of the television — did provide us with viewing options and also a promise. "Whomever I've loaned this DVD player to has gotten a heart within two weeks." I'll take two.

Yet another fabulous nurse loaned us her copy of *The Hangover*. Neither Jeremy nor I had heard of it, and we were almost reluctant to watch it. We caved at the diversion, of course, and, well, if you've seen *The Hangover* then you understand that we really enjoyed it, laughed even. My heart came less than two weeks later. We would joke that the DVD player should have been issued to me on admission to the hospital.

CHAPTER 34

NO, THE **HEART** IS BROKEN

Jeremy

At this point I had developed a permanent pain in my stomach. I was beginning to realize that Joclyn might not make it out of this room. I noticed our visitors' doubt more than before. I could see the look on their faces as they left. I could no longer eat a full meal. I started to imagine a life without Joclyn. I wondered what I would do if I lost her. Joclyn would notice I was distracted, but I would never tell her what I was thinking. I always assured Joclyn that she was going to be fine and a heart would come soon. It was early in the week around January 10th, that an X-ray technician came into the room to measure the activity in Joclyn's heart. After he wheeled in this giant device, he hooked Joclyn up with a bunch of wires using those sticky patches that were going to be a pain to take off. After a few minutes of confusion and watching him scratch his head, he declared that his machine was broken.

"What?" he said gently. He wanted to know what Joclyn just screamed at him in an inaudible whisper. I explained that his machine was not broken, and a machine cannot detect what is not there. "Her heart does not have any activity," I explained. The technician started to laugh and told us that he has been doing this for over 25 years. He explained that it was not possible for his machine to detect zero heart activity, and that his machine was malfunctioning. Joclyn and I both remained quiet and let him leave without argument. We both knew the truth and we were not going to waste our time. The next day he realized it was unlikely his machine had happened to malfunction again in this exact hospital room by coincidence. I was not there, but Joclyn told me he walked out of the room in shocked disbelief.

By this time, I was freaking out and felt like I was losing my mind. I was unable to eat and the pain in my stomach was getting worse. I was convinced Joclyn was down to her last days. The most recent round of chemo had made her weak, but I perceived that she was dying. I was no longer able to imagine her healthy again. I was convinced her heart was dead and there was no way she could survive on a machine much longer. When JoJo, the on-duty nurse, came into the room he noticed how white I was and asked me if I was okay. I told him of my concern and what had happened with the technician, and declared that her heart was dead and I needed to know how much time we had. JoJo pointed to the CentriMag device and told me that this was her heart. He explained that the machine was pumping her blood throughout her body, and that she was going to be fine. Just like Dr. Chen, he insisted that I forget about the heart in her chest, and told me it was going to be okay. JoJo was taking care of more than just his patient. He is a great nurse. He is one of my heroes.

All of a sudden it was January 11th and I realized that exactly 13 years ago I was on a plane moving to California to start a new life. I never would have guessed the road that lay ahead or that I would end up in the spot I was at that moment. How could I have known that I would eventually be a teacher back in New York City, married just six months, and already so close to burying my wife. It was a horrible thing to think, but sometimes we need to be honest with ourselves. I was hanging by a thread and I did not know how much longer I could put on the "it's going to be okay" act for Joclyn. We may have only been married for six months, but Joclyn knew that something was wrong. Instead of asking me about it she put her arms out for a hug. I reached in to hug her wanting to feel comforted by my wife who was 100% dependent on a machine for life. I noticed something for the first time since it had all started. Where did my wife go? She was there in front of me, but she was disappearing. Literally. I had just noticed how thin she had become. I could not believe I was just noticing how tiny she was. Her shoulders were disappearing. I think her swollen feet must have weighed more than the rest of her combined.

I pulled away and asked her where she was disappearing to. I realized I was crying. I could no longer put an act. I was worried and unsure of the future. I needed my best friend to know it. I needed to share how frightened I had become and how badly I felt we needed this heart to come. I was convinced she was running out of time. I started to fear the doctors and nurses were peddling false hope, and knew, as I did, that she was not going to make it. I knew that swollen feet was a deadly sign of heart failure. I thought the machines were starting to fail. I questioned how long a person could live without a heart because deep down I knew Joclyn's heart was dead. I had spent so much time trying to stay positive and convince everyone she was going to be all right, I needed someone to convince me. Joclyn recognized my needs, and assured me she was fine. She picked up my spirits and convinced me it would be all right.

I was feeling a little bit better thanks to Joclyn's positive attitude. It was Tuesday night, January 12th, three weeks since Joclyn was put on top of the transplant list. JoJo asked if he could speak with me outside the room. I went out with him and he told me he had an idea. He had asked around and found out that we could bring our dog Sedaris into the hospital lobby, and Joclyn could walk out to see her. I was very excited about this and knew it would make Joclyn incredibly happy to get this news. As JoJo walked away my excitement faded a bit, suddenly I began to convince myself this visit was to say goodbye. My stomach spun in circles as I tried to figure out another reason they would break hospital policy and allow my dog into the lobby of a cardiac unit. The more I thought about it the more I was convinced I was close to losing her. My mind again raced with pictures of what my life would become without her. I started to panic for her, and what she would feel like when she realized she had so little time left. I had to sit down. My mouth was dry. Luckily, it was cleanup time for Joclyn, so I had some time to recover.

When I went back into the room I had regained my composure. I stayed with Joclyn until about 11:00 that night. We talked about the upcoming weekend and how glad we were that it was Martin

Luther King Day that Monday, so we would have an extra day together. Joclyn made me promise that I would stay in the hospital the entire time and just bring a change of clothing. I agreed, and we focused on getting through the week. I dreaded leaving to go home each night. I became increasingly worried the phone would ring with horrible news whenever I was away from the hospital. The thought of a three-day weekend was a dream, because it meant not having to leave and face the fear of the phone.

Joclyn

Every morning, I was made to undergo a chest X-ray (bedside, of course, and it was up to me 50% of the time to remind the X-ray technician to cover my lady parts with the lead vest) and an echocardiogram. One day, the echocardiogram technician said that he could not detect any cardiac activity, and that he would have to come back tomorrow and try again. Perhaps my cell phone was nearby, he posited, or maybe his machine was just broken entirely. Jeremy and I looked at each other and both insisted that no, what he was seeing was my heart, not the result of any kind of interference. He did not seem to believe us, but when he returned the following day with a different machine that obtained the same non-readings as his first attempt, he looked at me sadly and slowly walked out, not saying a word. I guess no one had told him, either. He was sure I'd be dead by evening, I thought aloud. "Shhh." But Jeremy was unconvinced I would survive the day as well.

I was also attached to a standard heart monitor, the same as any patient in an ICU, and sometimes the alarms would go off. Usually someone would come running. Essentially, the alarms were ringing because they are supposed to ring when the person to whom they are attached does not have a detectable heart rate and rhythm. But we knew that I didn't have that. That's why I had had surgically implanted devices to take over. Still, even though the alarms were to ring pretty much all the time because of my condition, I was told by more than one nurse that it is "illegal" to turn them off. Other nurses frequently fretted over how to document their time with me. "I have to write a rate and rhythm. I don't know what to call this!" This is not the type of pioneering I'd ever imagined myself a part of. I was angered and confused by this constant panic because I was part of such a specialized program within the heart failure specialty at this hospital. Dr. Chen would many times walk through my door and tap the machines to which I was tethered and say, "THIS is your heart. Don't worry about the beeping." I baffled many, but rather than use common sense or engage what they'd learned about implantable ventricular devices, they instead assumed that the heart monitors were telling a true story about immediate peril, and acted as though I was pretty much always coding. One nurse wouldn't let me go to sleep one night, shaking me awake every time my eyes closed. Finally, one day, Dr. Horn wrote an order that allowed the volume to be turned down on my monitors.

Each device also had its own unique, blastingly-loud alarm, as if the entire situation wasn't frightening enough. Sometimes they would whinny, and that was truly terrifying, nothing like the heart monitors, since those really were doing the job of sending blood around my body. I don't think that they ever chimed for very long, though, as the cause was generally a kinked connection or perhaps I'd bore down too much while using the bedpan. Seriously. It happened. I did panic if someone didn't come rushing in to adjust whatever needed adjusting, though, and found it ironic that the heart monitors that meant nothing were diligently listened to. But the things that were actually keeping me alive were gotten around to when they were gotten around to. I sometimes felt like I lived on my nurse call button. Having worked in hospitals, I was at the same time impressed that said button was answered so quickly.

One day I noticed that the CentriMag alarm was ringing more than usual, and though it did silence when the machine was adjusted, we heard talk of a possible extra open-heart surgery to adjust the pumps. All Jeremy and I could think was, "This heart needs to come soon."

CHAPTER 35

DEXTER, INTERRUPTED

Jeremy

It was Thursday, and as I drove towards the hospital and I knew I was only a day of work away from that three-day weekend. Joclyn was in good spirits when I got there. We had a nice evening planned. Marc was coming to visit and stay for awhile and then Joclyn and I were going to watch *Dexter*. Joclyn made it clear to me she wanted to watch two episodes. She insisted it had to be two episodes. Watching *Dexter* was one of her highlights of the day, and I had no intention of arguing with this demand. When Marc showed up he mentioned he was hungry. We decided to order a pizza. We got Joclyn a salad, and everyone was in good spirits. I had actually forgotten my anxiety about how much time we had left and felt very relaxed. We spent some time joking around and eating. Life felt a little normal for a change.

After a while Leslie popped in the room. Rachel was with her. Joclyn was surprised to see them, but appreciated that they came in for a visit since they were in the city. Any awkwardness between Joclyn's parents had long departed by now. Everyone in Joclyn's life came together out of a common concern for her. After some time together, Marc left and headed home. Leslie waited for Jay to show up as he was out shooting billiards somewhere in the city. It took him a while to show up and Joclyn was getting frustrated. It was getting late and Joclyn was determined to squeeze (that's right, two) episodes of *Dexter* in that night. If Jay did not show up soon, she knew I would not be able to stay for both episodes. I still had one more day of work before the start of the three-day weekend. I was adamant about getting enough sleep to perform acceptably at work. Eventually, Jay showed up. Joclyn made it obvious she was anxious for them to leave. I felt bad pushing any visitor out the door, but my concern was to make Joclyn happy. Finally, they took the hint and cleared out. Joclyn and I were finally free for two episodes of murder and suspense.

Within five minutes of getting her mother out the door, I had the computer up and running and ready to play the next episode of *Dexter*. Even though it was going to keep me there past 11:00 p.m., I gave in and agreed to watch the two full episodes anyway. About 15 minutes into the first episode, a new nurse we had never seen before came into the room. I realized it was a little after 9:00 p.m., which meant it was time for the new nurse on duty to go through the check-up routine that usually required me to leave the room for 20–25 minutes. This made me groan as I realized I was going to end up staying well past 11:30 at this rate. I took off my headphones so I could hear what this new nurse was saying to us. I was a bit annoyed, and then surprised when she asked if she could speak with me outside the room. I did not know what that meant, but I was sure any really bad news would probably come from a doctor. So, I held back and allowed myself not to panic. Joclyn was quicker to question the nurse and insist on knowing why she had to speak to me in private.

"We just need Mr. Krevat to take a phone call and agree to accepting the new donor heart on Joclyn's behalf."

I noticed her begin to smile and could tell she was waiting to share this news with us, and she was originally following protocol when she entered the room. Joclyn's reaction was typical of her usual demeanor of late: "Are you fucking kidding with me? Are you serious?" The nurse did not seem to mind Joclyn's language or doubt. She just looked at me and waved me out of the room towards the phone. I kissed Joclyn and left the room. On my way out I stopped and turned towards Joclyn to ask, "Do you want this heart?" And I turned back to leave with the image of Joclyn smiling with tears welling in her eyes.

I grabbed the phone and heard a young female voice on the other end of the line:

Me: *Hello?*

Young female voice: *Hello, am I speaking with Jeremy Krevat?*

Me: *Yeah, I am me. (nervous laugh)*

Young female voice: *We have found a great heart for your wife.*

Me: *Great.*

Young female voice: *We need to confirm that you would like this heart.*

Me: *Confirmed. We want it.*

Young female voice: *OK. We will have the team at Columbia inspect and approve the heart in person. Congratulations, Mr. Krevat.*

Me: *Thank you, thank you so much.*

I hung up the phone and hurried back into the room with Joclyn. My mind was racing with what the next three hours was going to entail. Nurses I had spent the past seven weeks with were smiling and hugging me. They were telling me how happy they were and how glad they were to be on duty when the news came. The entire staff was buzzing and watching every move I made. I just wanted to get back to Joclyn and make sure this was real and I was not dreaming. Joclyn was smiling when I came into the room. She was excited and relieved. I realized she was thinking the same thing I was at that moment. There was finally a light at the end of the tunnel, a path to going home. I looked at her, and told her, based on the conversations I'd had with her doctors, when they told us she needed a transplant, that she would probably be home in three weeks. Joclyn quickly scolded me and insisted it would be two weeks. I was going to argue that with our luck it would take the full three weeks in the two to three-week estimate we were given, but decided to hold my tongue and agree that it would be only two weeks.

As people rushed in and out of the room I began gathering all of our stuff and packing it all up in bags. I was told we were going to leave in an hour. I knew I had to get all the gifts and gluten-free snacks packed up and into the car. I was glad I had the car by the hospital that day, but also had to think about how I would move it before the morning. A perfectly good spot at night is a spot that gets a car towed after 9:00 a.m. After making a plan in my head about how I would deal with the car, I realized I should probably be calling some people up and giving them the news. The first call I made was to Joclyn's father. Marc picked up the phone and knew why I was calling. He couldn't explain how; he just knew. I heard Cheryl scream in the background. He told me he would let everyone on Joclyn's side of the family know what was happening.

My parents were happy to get my call with the news of a new heart. They quickly sprang into action and called the rest of my family. Within minutes all of our family members were aware of what was happening. People were coming in and out of the room as Joclyn and I wept with a mix of happiness and fear in our hearts. In all the excitement it was easy to forget she was about to undergo a heart transplant. I promised her the worst was over and she would be fine, and I knew she would be fine. I knew it, and was as confident about it as I had ever been since this started. Joclyn was going to make it through this operation, and we were going to go home. I knew this with absolute certainty. I just did.

Suddenly Neshama came bursting into the room barking out orders to a bunch of nurses and other medical professionals who were lingering around. By this time, even after playfully referring to her as Dr. Gloom-and-Doom, she had become more than the expert on Joclyn's LVAD device. She had become a trusted friend. She was not on duty; she was not on call; she was there for Joclyn. She came because she was going to make sure that Joclyn's transfer to Columbia was a success. As the medical transport team arrived they discussed how she would be moved with all the machines and equipment that were keeping her heart pumping blood. The batteries that would power the machines in absence of electricity would give her about 45 minutes of power. Columbia was normally a 30-minute drive. There was a heavy backup generator that would provide a much longer guarantee of power that the EMS response unit was considering not bringing because of the bulk and weight. One of the guys said they would hurry and make it in plenty of time.

Neshama did not like this plan. She went from a very caring role to Joclyn, and converted back to the woman I first met a little over a month ago. Basically, this was one Israeli woman that you do not want to mess with. Her voice grew very deep and loud as she told them they WOULD be taking the backup generator that would guarantee up to four hours of power. The men did not argue with her; they quickly started loading the equipment without an ounce of objection. While they were packing up my wife, under the militant care of Neshama, I emailed my principal to tell her I would not be in the next day. I also mentioned that I would probably be in Tuesday if everything went smoothly, but I could not guarantee it. Looking back at it I cannot help but laugh at the things I felt needed to be done just hours before Joclyn's transplant. I guess I needed to keep myself busy.

The next thing I know I was riding up front in an ambulance with the lights flashing heading up the FDR. Joclyn would not hear of me bringing the car over separately. Every bump was scary. I almost told the driver to go slowly and steer around any bumps. Suddenly I looked up and saw Yankee Stadium. I screamed back to Joclyn to tell her I could see the stadium. Only months before the Yankees had won their 27th championship with the help of Joclyn's favorite player, Nick Swisher. I am not sure if she heard me at the time, but it felt great to see something that reminded me of our lives before all of this happened. Winning the championship just months before this ordeal, the Yankees gave Joclyn a great thrill. I celebrated with her that night remembering how great it felt in 1986 when the Mets won it.

My cell phone buzzed and interrupted my thoughts about baseball. I looked down at my phone and saw a text message from Frank and Jenny asking how Joclyn was doing. I was not sure how they knew what was happening, but assumed it may have gone viral by now due to a family member posting on CaringBridge. I was surprised to find out that it was merely a coincidence and they both had just returned from a trip and were just checking in. Frank and Jenny are professors at Brooklyn College, and Joclyn actually took Frank's class years before. They developed a lasting friendship. I explained what was happening and where we were. I will never forget their reply: Frank and Jenny wanted to come to the hospital at 12:00 a.m. and wait with me all night in the waiting room. I told them I could not ask them to do that, but they insisted and informed me they were already calling the cab. I was and will always be grateful.

As we arrived at the Columbia parking lot I was anxious to get out of the vehicle and get to the back to see Joclyn. As they opened the back doors and pulled her out with all the equipment, Joclyn's eyes lit up in excitement. I forgot how long it had been since she had felt and breathed in fresh outside air. It was Manhattan air; it was cold, but she clearly appreciated the moment, real weather. When she was loaded for the trip to Columbia, the back of the ambulance was right by the back door of the hospital; Joclyn did not get to be outside. When we arrived at Columbia, we were a good 20 yards from the front door. Then everything almost came to an end as the men lowering Joclyn down from the back of the vehicle dropped the stretcher to a crashing thud. Neshama who was in the back with Joclyn the whole time quickly checked the equipment, as I tried to swallow my stomach that had suddenly jumped to the top of my throat, "if you get into a small car accident, she dies." Luckily, Joclyn was fine and all the equipment was functioning normally. Just minutes later we were upstairs being moved into a small room in the intensive care unit.

Joclyn

Harking back to *Dexter,* again, the real significance of this show in our lives is, besides that it sustained our sanity to a strong degree while waiting for the heart, it was also on during the news of receiving a heart! Season One, Episode Nine, to be specific, thanks to Netflix's "viewing history" option. Creepy, actually. Just looking at that backdated queue gives me the heebie-willies, knowing that those dates all correspond to my life support imprisonment. Some are After, but that part of being institutionalized was miserable torture as well. I have decided hereafter to not look at that list again.

We were early on in watching Season One, Episode Nine of *Dexter*, having just finished Episode Eight, secured in our spots with headphones. We had just thrown out my mother and her husband and were finally alone. A nurse whom I'd never "had" before came in, excitedly, at around shift change time, and I didn't hear what she'd said immediately because of the headphones. "What?" She needed to speak to Jeremy. *Uh, oh,* we probably both thought.

What's the problem? She could barely contain herself. "I need you to come to the phone and speak to so-and-so because Columbia has a heart!" The phone didn't reach, and neither could I, hence the need for Jeremy, my "proxy," my "next of kin," my oh my.

Jeremy told me that I shouted, hoarsely, an emphatic "Are you fucking kidding me?" I remember crying for about two seconds, also. I covered my mouth. Jeremy demanded to know how I could think that a nurse — other than the one who asked me if I wanted to die — could be kidding about that. My thoughts immediately shifted to my standing, terrified thoughts of awakening during surgery thanks to that recent Chuck Scarborough clip, "Waking up during surgery, unable to speak or move. Could it happen to you?" Why, yes. Yes! Yes, that would definitely be the exact style of thing to happen to me. In fact, now that you've mentioned it, Chuck, my thoughts are consumed by this fear; it is the center of my consciousness, and I'm wondering, calculatingly, if just dying would be better than going through with this and risking actually feeling with my nerves what being operated on is like. Thanks for asking.

I was instantly more scared than ever of being alone. Because of the CentriMag and LVAD clot risks, I was on heparin, a blood thinner. Because of this, and in conjunction with the horrifically recycled dry hospital air I was forced to respirate exclusively, my nose bled at least daily, and was now bleeding again. I was worried that they wouldn't perform the transplant if my nose was bleeding. I was also worried that they would, but that I would choke to death on my nose blood, or that maybe I would wake up, choking on nose blood, unable to move or speak, with a sterile blue thing over my face and my chest open, no heart inside. How the fuck did I get here again?

I would be transported via ambulance to Columbia, in Washington Heights. By the way, that's exactly where I went to occupational therapy school. I liked it better there the first time around, seriously. But had you asked me at that time what I thought, as a student, I would have told you that I could have done without it. I'd have had no idea what really I could do without.

Jeremy gave me a choice. He could ride with me in the ambulance or he could load up the car with all of my stuff — much stuff had accumulated by that point — and take it all back to

Brooklyn and meet me at Columbia. We both knew that tons of waiting would be involved, and that the car to Brooklyn option made the most logical sense. But there was nothing logical about my need for him to stay near me for as long as possible. I wondered silently and wistfully if he could sit in on the transplant, even. What if I woke up during? He rode with me, although he was in the front passenger seat and we couldn't talk to each other. He told me later that he pointed out Yankee Stadium. I would have liked to hear that.

Neshama came as well. I was VERY impressed that she rushed in, from some type of painting class near her home in New Jersey, and I smiled hugely when I saw her appear in the hallway. She had been running and was out of breath! As LVAD coordinator for the hospital, she really wanted to make sure that the transfer went smoothly. She probably also wanted to make sure that Weill Cornell got their LVAD and CentriMag back. Sterilized or not, I found it difficult and ridiculous to imagine those pumps inside another person's body, saving his or her life as well.

It was to my extreme benefit that she was there. The EMTs were perfectly content to move me on battery power alone, but the CentriMag's battery only lasts for 45 minutes. "But it's a very close drive from 68th and York to 168th and Broadway." Her look spoke millions of words. I was certainly not comfortable with that. An accident or traffic for any reason could always happen; were these people for real? Neshama demanded. The backup generator came with us.

These same EMTs dropped my stretcher on exiting. I wasn't quite as horrified as Neshama — her eyes popped out of her head like a French bulldog with a thyroid condition. Because I was completely giddy about the exposure to fresh air, I didn't even care that it was freezing outside. Air!

I was pushed inside and brought to the cardiac intensive care unit, which immediately seemed sparser and less friendly than its counterpart at Weill Cornell. It seemed yellow. I noticed this while parked near a nurses' station waiting for Neshama to finish up with the EMTs and the whatnot of transferring custodial rights of a patient, or whatever loose ends need to be tied before one hospital can officially give a patient over to another.

CHAPTER 36

FINALLY

Jeremy

After filling out some paperwork, and answering about a million questions I had already answered about 100 times in the past month, I was told I would have to leave the area. I would get to return before the operation. The nursing staff back at Weill Cornell told me the operation was scheduled for 2:00 a.m. Neshama showed me to the waiting area as she said hello to people she used to work with at Columbia. She was clearly at home there and knew her way around. Her familiarity there eased my anxiety. I was feeling pretty good considering the night that lay ahead. Texts were coming in from my family. They all wanted updates and were letting me know they were with me in spirit. I thought of my friend Zachary Hayes as I read the word spirit. I decided to give him a call. It was still a reasonable time to call California, and he was my most religious close friend. He had flown out six months before to stand with me at my wedding. He was always a reliable friend when I lived across the street from him during my time in San Jose.

When Zach answered the phone I was concerned I woke up his kids, but he told me was just putting his oldest son Ben to bed and saying a prayer. I told him what was happening. He asked me if he could say a prayer with his family with me on the phone. I am not a religious person, but I was in tears by the time he was finished. His words were powerful and from the heart. I realized once again that I was not alone. After he was finished I thanked him and told him I would be in touch when everything was calm. Zach thanked me for calling. He told me he and the whole family would keep us in their prayers. I hung up the phone and waited in the lobby. I thought about the evening ahead. I could not believe how much had happened in the past four hours, and how fast everything was taking place.

I was glad to see Frank and Jenny arrive in the waiting room. Only one obstacle remained between Joclyn and this heart: the transplant team, after inspecting the heart, could reject it. Unfortunately, this is not an uncommon occurrence. I remembered the physician's assistants at Weill Cornell preparing us for this possibility. The arrival of Frank and Jenny distracted me from those thoughts. It was only a few minutes before the nurses came and said I could go back in and see Joclyn. They only allowed two people in the ICU at Columbia, so Frank hung back and Jenny came inside with me. When we got there Joclyn saw us coming and gave me a thumbs up. I knew that this was her way of telling me the heart was approved and they would be going ahead with the transplant. When I told Jenny, she did not question my interpretation. She just smiled and nodded. We kept Joclyn company while they prepared her for surgery. It was about 1:30 a.m., so we were getting very close.

At that point things moved fast. Jenny went back to the waiting room as they prepared Joclyn for surgery. Before I knew it, Frank came in for a quick hello and they were wheeling her away towards the elevator. That was as far as I was allowed to go. Joclyn was visibly frightened. She asked me to sing for her. I had to squash my gut reaction which was a huge "no way!" I struggled to figure out a song I could sing at that moment and ended up selecting "Moonshiner" by Uncle Tupelo, an impossible song to sing on key without Joclyn's guitar accompaniment. (She used to play this song for me often.) Joclyn did not seem to mind and as I struggled with the chorus as we came to the elevator. As I held back my tears because I did not want Joclyn to see my anxiety. I choked out an "I love you" and a "you will be fine." Joclyn let go of my hand and whispered out a goodbye, the loudest she could with her damaged vocal cords. As the elevator doors closed, I let the tears that were being held back free and headed towards the waiting room. I felt helpless.

At about 3:00 a.m. I decided to go back to Weill Cornell and get all of our things, and bring the car over to Columbia as I was in a tow away zone and did not have the option of waiting until morning. I took a cab. As I walked towards the room the nurses smiled at me and wished me the best of luck. A few of them told me how wonderful we were, and how I needed to keep them posted on Joclyn's condition. I thanked them all and collected our belongings, or at least the 75% of them that were packed up and in a closet. The remaining possessions are somewhere in a hidden hospital closet hiding and gone forever. Nothing was of very high value, so I did not make a huge investigation; I was in a rush to get back to Columbia. I said my goodbyes and drove back to the hospital. I found a parking spot that was legal until 6:00 a.m. I made a mental note to return and find a permanent parking spot for the day. But for the moment, it was a good spot that would get me back into the waiting room quickly.

I knew I was in for a long night when I got back and sat down with Frank and Jenny. The waiting room was empty with the exception of a Chinese woman who was basically living in the room. She had pillows and blankets and lots of luggage. A custodian explained that she had a daughter with a heart condition, and had not left the hospital since they came into the emergency room. This was her fifth night in the waiting room. She had already figured out a system of survival that appeared quite efficient. We all settled in as I set my alarm for 5:50 a.m., so I would have time to get to my car and find a parking lot to put it in. As I tried to sleep I felt a blanket being draped over me. I looked up to see the Chinese woman telling me I needed to stay warm. It is amazing how much a simple act of kindness could mean when done in certain moments of your life. I will never forget it, or her.

In what felt like a few seconds later my eyes opened to the sound of my alarm. I jumped up and headed to my car. Everyone else was sleeping, so I quietly left hoping not to disturb my friends, or the wonderful and dedicated mother across the room. I found a parking lot across the street from McDonald's. I ran over and ordered about ten random breakfast sandwiches after parking. It had seemed like forever since I had eaten, and my stomach was roaring for food. Knowing that Frank and Jenny were very good cooks who had a strong appreciation for gourmet food, I was not sure they would be interested in this bounty. Jenny shocked me when she lit up and said, "We love this stuff." I saved some for my new friend as well, but when she woke up she disappeared into the ICU. We ate and spoke about Joclyn. Time flew by quickly.

At about 7:00 a.m. a surgeon entered the room and approached us. As every organ in my body came into my throat, I confirmed to him that I was Mr. Krevat. "Your wife is doing great; the new heart started beating right away with no issues at all. We are about to close her up." He told me his name too, but at that point everything was a blur. He walked away. I turned to see Jenny crying. I realized I was crying as well. We hugged. Frank, who had left to get coffee, entered the room as the surgeon departed. He found Jenny and me in an embrace, in tears. We quickly signaled the thumbs up to him. His eyes began to water as well. He joined us, and we formed a group hug. We smiled and stood together for awhile, relieved at the news. After a few minutes, Frank and Jenny started gathering their belongings. They had to head out to work and settle back in after their vacation. I said my goodbyes, and got on the phone to update everyone.

As I texted everyone, not thinking they would be up, I found out my entire family was up all night waiting for news. It was still 4:00 a.m. in California. Lee, my dedicated and nervous brother, was up to receive the text because he never went to bed. He quickly responded that he would let everyone know the news, and I should keep him updated. I told him to be cautious as we were not out of the woods yet. They still had to close her up and carefully monitor her to make sure everything went well. I did not know if she was really in any more danger at the moment, but I did not want to jinx anything by declaring "Finished!" too soon. As the morning dragged on, Marc showed up in the waiting room. He looked exhausted. I had texted him right after texting Lee, and he was not sleeping either. At some point, Dr. Horn showed up in the waiting room and told me she happened to be in the building and thought she would stop by to see how everything was going. Before she left she told me that Joclyn's heart was more damaged and dysfunctional than any heart she had ever seen in a living person.

Minutes turned to hours and we were getting no word from anyone. I had people from all over the country texting me like crazy desperate for an update, but there was no update to give. It was 12:00 p.m. now, and it had been five hours since the last update. I realized this was a different and stricter hospital than Weill Cornell. After Joclyn's past surgeries I had been allowed in her room before her breathing tube was out. I started to wonder if this was not permitted at Columbia. I worried for Joclyn because I played such a big role in motivating her to breathe on her own after the last surgery. I feared that since she was alone, she would be unable to breathe well enough to convince the nurses it was safe to remove the breathing tube. But I waited, and so did everyone else. I could feel the tension in the texts I was getting. Nobody understood why it had been so long since the last update. I kept reassuring everyone that there was no news and I would keep them posted.

At 1:30 p.m., I lost it. I was too tired and weak to fight with doctors and nurses, so I sent Marc into the ICU to demand an explanation of where she was. I remember sternly telling him to go in there and demand to know what is happening to his daughter. He did not argue; he went. A few minutes later he came back to confirm she was back in her little room and they were waiting to remove the breathing tube. I felt a bit better, but was still shaken about how many hours had passed. About 15 minutes later, as Ellen and Carrie arrived to show support, I decided to do something drastic. I decided to bring my car home to Brooklyn, take a shower, and come back by train. This would kill a lot of time, and I needed to get away and make myself feel clean again. I headed to the car and hurried home for Brooklyn. My brother was in meetings at work in California by this time. He was actually announcing updates to his co-workers who were now fully invested like family members.

Joclyn

A doctor came to greet me; he may have shaken my hand. I was supine, so it could not have been an impressively firm one. He was introduced as the director of the transplant program, possibly, to which I replied, "Finally." He smiled and said, too, "Finally."

I waited and waited in what could easily have been mistaken for a holding cell of sorts, but it was my new room from that moment until a few days post-transplant. I was made to wait there until the donor heart could be examined and positively designated for my body. It wasn't a go for certain until the team laid eyes on it.

Not only was the Columbia ICU smaller and yellower than Weill Cornell, it also had a much less friendly visitors policy. It was more like a We'd Rather You Didn't Have Visitors Policy. First off, I was only allowed two visitors at a time. At Weill Cornell, I can remember having five people in my room at once with room for more. Second, the visitors could never get too comfortable. If anything happened to any other patient on the unit, all visitors were made to leave not just my room, but the entire corralling area and go outside a locked door without an explanation or indication of when they might be allowed to return.

If nothing out of the ordinary went on, and all was smooth, visitors could be asked to leave on a moment's notice. Regular hours were sporadic, and no sign was posted. I believe no one was allowed before 11 a.m. as a standing rule.

(These rules also applied during surgery, as in, if family members had a loved one in surgery say, being fitted with a just plucked donor heart, the family members' queries were best answered if they coincided with the unwritten but heavily restricted visiting hours, unposted as they were. We were not informed of this on admission.)

I waited in my cell, and soon learned that my dear friends Frank and Jenny had rushed over all the way from Brooklyn on learning that my new heart had come. It was a chance text message, a quick "How's she doing?" that prompted them to come and keep Jeremy company during the time that I could not keep him company as my chest would be open and I would be asleep in a special room designed for chests to be opened.

I was alone when a suited medical professional stuck her head into my curtained area and told me that the heart was suitable, and the transplant surgery would definitely happen. I may have cried for a moment. Jeremy and Jenny came in, since Frank was not allowed as he'd be a third wheel infringing on the two-at-a-time-like Noah's-ark policy. As they approached I gave a thumbs-up. (My voice was still quite hoarse from the multiple intubations and extubations that occur during open-heart surgeries, and closed heart, and probably most other surgeries.) Jenny put her hands to her mouth and did the excited emotional spin-around, which might have made me shed a tear or so, and Jeremy hung back, smiling by the curtain. It may have rubbed his cheek since he was leaning in rather than having stepped in.

It was a gigantic pain in the ass for visitors to enter my room. (It had been for them at Weill Cornell as well, but in all matters of humanity Weill Cornell was more lenient.) Hospitals are not clean like you might think. Operating rooms are kept sterile, but the rest of the hospital is not. Hospital-borne infections are a very real danger to people who are already sick, and it is a real struggle to contain them. Because a swab-of-my-nose test — which I could not recall having submitted to — revealed that I had MRSA, as in, Medically-Resistant Staphylococcus Aurcus, as in, Everyone Who Has Ever Worked in a Hospital Has This, all visitors to my room-slash-cubicle had to don a yellow (more yellow) gown, and put on non-latex gloves. This was a production.

Jeremy must have been hesitant to involve himself in the production right at that moment, but for me it seemed the moment was perfect for a bit of touchy togetherness. I motioned excitedly with my hand, and did so again. Jenny did laugh and say to Jeremy that she thinks I wanted him to come a little closer. Jenny retreated from the Rules Area; Frank came and probably blew a kiss followed by a rather encouraging statement, and left Jeremy and I alone.

The time came; my little area was crowded, and my nose started bleeding. It had been doing that a lot over the past few weeks. As I've mentioned, it must have been a combination of the Coumadin (blood thinning medication) and the snappily dry forced hospital air of which I'd been stuck breathing nothing but that made my membranes sensitive.

Instantly, I was reminded that I would likely choke to death on my own nose blood during the surgery. I tried to express this to the blue-scrubbed physician's assistant who was helping in the getting me to the operating room process, but she laughed at me. "You're worried about your nose?" I tried to silently tell Jeremy to remember that she said that when she later informed him that I'd choked to death on my own nose blood.

My other recurrent fear worthy of recurrent mention was of course the "I Will Wake Up During Surgery and be Paralyzed and Unable to Speak or Otherwise Emote" fear, which no one took seriously, either. I think I was actually terrified that that would happen. I told no one. I'd already told people about that one.

Jeremy was allowed to walk next to me as I was wheeled down the hallway to the bank of elevators that were off-limits to people who didn't work there, or who, if they didn't work there, were not about to have things done to their bodies that would require general anesthesia. I whispered that he should please sing to me.

He sang to me. He sang "Moonshiner," the traditional folk song that we best knew as an Uncle Tupelo cover. The pressure must have really been on, because I am confident that there are not many other circumstances in which I could direct my husband to sing and have him comply with only minimal hesitation.

We arrived at the elevators, and the pushers of my trolley told him he'd have to turn back. I still wonder what would have happened had he refused. Would we have stood there all night, indefinitely postponing the surgery, engaged in a Jewish standoff? Either way, Jeremy turned back. He leaned way down and kissed me. I wished and continued to wish he could somehow stay with me.

I may have told Jeremy I was scared before he walked away. Charlene later told me that I sent her a text message, as I was being transferred, that I was scared.

I do not remember the elevator ride down, but I do remember waiting in a hallway outside of the operating room.

On being wheeled in, as everyone being prepped for surgery probably does, I stared at the lights on the ceiling. I didn't look at the people because they did not return the favor, ensuring even greater unease. I saw people unwrapping tools, and this I did not need (see previous fear of awakening). I was made to transfer from my trolley to a very narrow operating table. Are they always so impossibly narrow? Is the alternative only a bariatric table with a 500 lb. weight minimum to satisfy the requirements of that particular billing code?

I asked none of these questions as an oxygen mask was tourniqueted to my face — and removed when I protested that it was a tad tight — and a drip of Versed was started. I had a PICC line in my arm which I was told would not be used, but rather removed, and the narcotics began to flow through my standard IV. Pain due to collapsed veins be damned, it was assumed that this did not matter as I'd be asleep in no time. This sounded wonderful to me, relatively speaking, until panic mildly ensued when the assistant surgeon, Dr. Ghaly, realized that I had not yet signed the consent. I had not yet given written permission for my donor's heart to be transplanted into my body. This is key. Operating without explicit permission is felony assault at best. Permission granted while under the influence of narcotics does not count.

My fear of prematurely awakening from anesthesia was momentarily replaced by a fear that the heart would go to waste and I would be returned to Weill Cornell.

"Quick, just sign this."

"The Versed has already been started, doctor."

Dr. Ghaly ignored the voice and shoved a pen into my hand. Maybe they thought I would forget, after. Or they maybe just assumed that I would never accuse them of assault.

Jeremy later confirmed that he was pretty sure that he would have been contacted to sign as my proxy rather than have the entire procedure abandoned. Good hearts are hard to come by. I would later learn that four of them had been turned down by the transplant team on my behalf before this awesome day. Relatively.

CHAPTER 37

UP

Jeremy

After showering and leaving for the hospital I waited for the train, and began to panic. This was taking longer than I expected. What if she wakes up and I am not there? What if something goes wrong? Suddenly, I was shaking in anticipation, waiting impatiently for the train to start moving again after each stop. When I got out of the subway and headed towards the entrance of the hospital I saw Ellen and Carrie. They saw me and screamed, "She is up!" They handed me their visitor pass so I would not have to wait in line for another one. I raced upstairs and into the ICU towards her room. I sent one last text to Lee, telling him she was up and I was heading in. He responded with a simple "yay." I turned towards Joclyn and saw Marc there, looking ten years younger than I had seen him all month. And there was Joclyn, wide awake and smiling at me.

As I called Lee on the phone to tell him she was awake and talking to me he began to laugh, and cry. He kept repeating the same thing over and over again: "She just had a heart transplant, and she is — awake. And. Talking." All I could think to do was remind him that her definition of talking was a scratchy whisper. I explained to Joclyn where I had been, and that I was refreshed, and not going to leave her unless they kicked me out. She was just happy to see me. Then I took a few minutes to appreciate that the huge CentriMag machine, and the four giant red tubes going in and coming out of her, were gone. She still had plenty of tubes going in and out of her, but there was certainly nothing mechanical in her that was responsible for the beating of her heart. It was the most miraculous sight I had ever laid eyes on. My wife up and awake, with a functioning heart.

Joclyn

Regularly visiting hospitals, any of them, does not preclude the need to stop at the security desk, declare who the visited patient is, and take the offering of a pass. Much like a hall pass from public school, it implies permission granted for something not typically allowed without special arrangement. Because Jeremy visited daily, it didn't take long for him to learn and master the system behind the system.

Before the transplant, at Weill Cornell, a visitor's pass was not needed. Company only needed to show identification to be permitted entry beyond the security station. Columbia, however, had a color-coded daily changing pass system, and at times, I understand, the line for one could become quite long. There was also the two-visitor-per-patient policy — a sensible policy in the instance of a patient who shares a room, but what about someone like me in intensive care who has a cell all to herself? A Rolodex-style folder system ensured that there were never too many visitors per patient space, but, similar to my question regarding the limitation, I also felt compelled to ask Jeremy what of the times when a leaving visitor did not return the pass? Certain visitors were known to have thrown hers away, left it behind, or otherwise rendered it inaccessible.

Jeremy keenly beat the system by creating a collection of visitor's passes. He had one of each color, as well as the sometimes-used smaller version that had a map on one side, gently folded and kept inside the pockets of his winter jacket. This may have been more difficult to pull off if it had been warmer outside.

He would take a quick glance around, note the color of the day, and stealthily pull the appropriate one from his coat and saunter in like he owned the place. I was up in my room during these processes, of course, but I like to imagine that the walk in was a stealthy saunter. We may have started this hospitalization in non-questioning fear, but the minutiae of what the rent-a-cops say we can do inside my room/temporary home, rules made by people who could not possibly live our lives for a single day, those rules we had become quite comfortable with ignoring.

There were several instances where for one reason or another this tactic did not work, and a visitor's pass relay race-style handoff took place near the security desk. Friends were made to wait to visit on occasion.

Weekends are always precious, and to my friends who work, giving up part of their valuable time away from their jobs was an enormous sacrifice. It really bothered me that sometimes their limited time was wasted having to wait for a visitor's pass.

CHAPTER 38

HURRY! EAT!

Jeremy

Now that the transplant was complete, we started to become familiar with our new surroundings. We moved from a huge room in intensive care at Weill Cornell to a tiny cubicle with no windows, and certainly no extra bed for me to sleep on. The nurses were a lot more intense as well. They were all Filipino, and kept yelling at me that I was in their way every time they came into the room. My attempt at charming them, saying "hello' and "thank you" in their native Tagalog, got me nowhere. One phrase I remembered in Tagalog, from a few years earlier, was "Shut up, you stupid idiot boy." This did not elicit even a hint of a smile from these nurses. These women were serious. (And short.)

The rules were much stricter as well. I could no longer be in the cubicle with Joclyn whenever I wanted. They had specific hours. Every time there was a medical emergency in the unit, they tossed me out into the waiting area. There was a phone in the waiting area, and they would call the phone and tell people it was alright to come back in. The problem was that people would run to answer the phone. If it was not a call for them, they would neglect to make sure the message got out to the correct person. I resorted to calling the nurses' station myself, which must have driven them crazy, but I did not care. I also got busted with a cell phone in the cubicle. One nurse told me the presence of my cell phone explained why Joclyn's external pacemaker, which every heart transplant patient requires after his or her surgery, was malfunctioning. I doubted her, until I shut off my phone and Joclyn's pacemaker started functioning normally. DOH!

The food at Columbia was worse as well. As bad as we thought it was at Weill Cornell, at least there we knew what she was being served. We were lucky we could identify the food there because the man who delivered it was certainly not going to take the time to tell us. He was a bitter man who came into the room with an angry energy. We actually got to a point that I was nervously clearing room for the food so I did not have to deal with his reaction to a crowded bed tray. The sooner he put the food down in front of her, the sooner he would be out of our lives until the next meal. By taking the items Joclyn wanted from the tray, then placing the tray outside the door, we eliminated the need to deal with him after mealtime. That way, we avoided his impatience with Joclyn's slow pace of eating, and avoided his general unpleasantness as well.

Joclyn

When I worked in a nursing home, a patient once replied with a snarky "whore baths" when I asked as part of her occupational therapy assessment how she took care of her personal hygiene. Having never before experienced such a turn of phrase, I may have laughed with her. However, I did decipher instantly that she was implying that the cheap freshness supposedly obtained via sponging off with warm water and threadbare washcloths while sitting bedside was similar to the method probably used by prostitutes who have lined up back-to-back clients and haven't the time for the technicalities of proper bathing.

The reader will recall that pre-transplant, my hygiene routines were pretty much handled for me. Post-transplant, at Columbia, my routine became a whore bath combined with a less than generous offer from nursing assistants with attitudes to "help with [my] back and feet but we don't do private parts." Not that I wanted anyone with an attitude touching my lady parts, but I didn't want to be told that I was officially on my own. I didn't go through withdrawal. But I thought, for some reason, that it seemed unfair.

I am eternally grateful that my time spent waiting for a heart was at Weill Cornell, and not Columbia. My team at Weill Cornell explained to me, and I do agree, that Columbia feels more like a public hospital, while Weill Cornell has the pampered feel of private industry to it.

Take meal service. Good Moooorning, Ms. Krevat (Nice Food Lady would pronounce it Krev-it), as she came in with Rice Chex each morning. (Rice Chex, at the time, was pretty much the only mainstream gluten-free cereal, and although never officially listed on the menu that was tossed in my direction each morning, it somehow usually made it to my tray.) I guess I was hooked up, in the dietary department, by one of the many people who probably felt really bad for me. Maybe it was the rheumatologist with no bedside manner who would later tell me, post-transplant, that I'd gotten a heart just in time and may not have lived another week if I hadn't. She and her boss had repeatedly stressed the importance to my recovery of eating right. It was also kind of horrible when Nice Food Lady would come in, however. While it may have been the beginning of her workday, and she had that *je ne sais quois* pep in her step for me, or anyone on life support, for me it felt like a rude awakening from a terrible night's sleep.

Night time was often not really a time for hours of restful slumber. Even with the amazing drugs, I often did not fall asleep before one a.m., and there were doctors and phlebotomists prancing in and assaulting me starting from around 5:00 a.m. Didn't they understand that restful sleep is necessary for health? I had a firm grasp on that nugget well before ever working in healthcare, pre life support.

(Re: life support, I mean, I was never on a ventilator, thank God, but I was certainly on machines which sustained my life to the point that when they alarmed, one or two people would drop what they were doing and come running.)

The food delivery lady was very nice, and I'd even like to visit her, and tell her I am well now, but it was just nothing short of brutal torture when, after finally falling back asleep after some early morning bodily attack to have someone so loud and jarring come in and subtly make me feel lousy if I didn't return the greeting with an equal enthusiasm, and a profound thanks for having delivered my breakfast.

There was an older gentleman who was her alter ego. He was not nice; quite grumpy, in fact. He used to come in and put down my food tray in an impatient way, and would only express a salutation if pushed into it by an exuberantly friendly Jeremy. He would express angry frustration if the lights in my room were not on fully, and would threaten to leave even before he entered. If a space for tray plopping was not prepared on his arrival, that too was a catastrophe for him. His impending arrival caused stress. I actually remember Jeremy panicking over there not being enough exposed space on my bedside table or environs and snapping at visitors.

"Don't put that there! The food guy is going to come and get mad if he can't put down the tray within two seconds of entering!"

This dietary worker also always came back to take my tray well before I'd finished, and this habit of his seemed to him to be a reflection on me, and was very off-putting to him. I read all of this from his expression, even straight through his dark glasses. It was as if he was not a paid employee assigned with the task of delivering putrid, nauseating slop to people in cardiac intensive care units who were bed-bound and attached to various life-sustaining devices, but rather that he was a person who, in his spare time, chose to deliver delicious, artisanal meals to the strong and able-bodied, all of whom snatched the wares from his hand, blew smoke in his face, and snapped at him to touch nothin' on his way out. And not to mention that the food was barely edible to begin with. 90% of the time I ate maybe one thing off the tray, and Jeremy was left with the task of finding food for me that might actually have had a USDA "fit for human consumption" label printed on its ingredients at some stage in its preparation.

The joke almost was on us, though, because the food at Weill Cornell was heaps better than at Columbia. We didn't realize this immediately, as my first non-vile non-broth meal post-transplant was some kind of non-shellfish paella knockoff that I swear I remember as being kind of tasty, if not a bit unseasoned. The nurse, Lissy — Indian, she said — laughed when we told her that I quite enjoyed it. Every single meal that followed during my month there was so nauseatingly inappropriate that I would literally beg the food delivery person not to enter my room with the sludge. Even with the lid on the plate, the smell — all of the food smelled like cooked athlete's foot combined with some kind of spoiled fish — would close my throat and clench my stomach, often to the point of actual vomit. These delivery people were so unempathetic that they would never just not deliver it. "No, I gotta" was often what they mumbled, perhaps under orders from the pharmacy, as the more I gagged, the more Zofran I would request, and the more they could charge my insurance company. I have no proof of this theory, obviously. But doesn't it make sense, even if you aren't disposed to subscribe to conspiracy theories?

The takeout food options were more numerous at Weill Cornell than at Columbia. The Upper East Side of Manhattan is pretty tony, so while it remained as much of a challenge to find reasonably-priced fare, as it would have if we were in that neighborhood during the course of normal life, options still existed. We took our recommendations from the nursing staff. Sushi, barbecue, Chinese, burgers: pretty much what someone in New York City would want to eat versus cook in their tiny kitchens or, in my case, what I would choose to eat over the nauseating hospital provisions, and what also could have possibly at any moment become my last meal. Before we learned from the nurses that food delivery was possible, Jeremy thought he had to leave the hospital to go get food, limiting us to a four-block radius. This was both because it was winter, and also because traveling a greater distance than that would mean more time apart. We were both willing to sacrifice our food quality a little bit to avoid that. Ever nervous, though, because the restaurant delivery people would only venture into the hospital as far as the lobby, Jeremy would head down early to meet them there. This still resulted in unnecessary time apart because Jeremy would always want to go to the lobby well before the delivery person called. I gave up asking him why he didn't just wait for them to call; he said that sometimes the elevators took a long time. I don't doubt that they did, but I still was stressed by his absence. Maybe I was a little bit too needy.

CHAPTER 39

A STEP DOWN IS A STEP UP

Jeremy

Everything went smoothly for the 48 hours post-surgery. Slowly, different tubes were removed. The nurses started to calm down a bit. We would not be in the intensive care unit much longer. There was talk that Joclyn would be moved to a regular room known as a step-down room if everything stayed on track. It was Sunday and I had the Monday off thanks to the great activist Martin Luther King Jr. It was also the day of an important playoff game. The Jets were set to play the San Diego Chargers and were a big underdog in the game. I had seen the Jets beat the Chargers in the playoffs a couple of years earlier, so I held out hope they could pull off the upset again. I stood next to my wife staring into a ten-inch, static-filled television set screaming my brains out and carrying on like a maniac at every bad play. I behaved like this only 48 hours after Joclyn received a new heart. Joclyn did not really mind, and she actually joined in. The nurses, however, looked like they were going to throw me into a pot of adobo to stew. The Jets won the game. The next day Joclyn was moved to the step-down unit. I was shocked to walk in and find her with only one IV bag attached to her arm. I could hug my wife again.

When I returned to work on Tuesday, I was a new man. I had gone from a stress case always checking my phone to see if a heart had come, to a husband counting the days until his wife could come home. When the English class I co-taught with Mr. Olearchik (Mr. O) began, we started the period with our normal pleasantries that would always follow a weekend off from school. As some of the students shared their activities from the past few days, Mr. O announced to the class that my wife had gotten a new heart and was doing great. I guess I had not realized how aware the students were of my situation at that moment because they broke out in a huge celebration of applause and screaming approval. It was overwhelming. I fought back tears. I had no idea so many students knew about my ordeal.

I also taught a class that is referred to as a "Resource Room." This is where students who needed extra help would work with me in a smaller setting, and it provided the opportunity for catching up on subjects in which they were struggling. Within a month of the class, our group grew as some of the other 9th graders wanted in on our little community. A few of the girls, who were close friends with one another, were curious about my life. They would always ask me questions about myself, and about my wife. This had to be the source of how the details of my life became public knowledge amongst all the students.

This curiosity of the students began before Joclyn was sick. I shared stories with them, and believed that they would benefit from seeing a wider panorama, beyond their own families, of adult life. They always loved to hear what my wife and I would do on the weekends. The fact that Joclyn and I didn't have any children of our own fascinated them. I started to make a strong connection to these students, and began to understand how that would benefit me as a teacher when trying to teach students from different backgrounds than my own.

One of my students, whom I will just call "Judy," had a very witty and funny personality. One thing I loved most about her was her desire to connect with and ingratiate herself with teachers. She would tell each of us separately that we each were her favorite teacher. After Joclyn got sick the students saw a change in me and started to ask questions. I told them about my wife and Judy started to cry. She demanded to talk to my wife, and I broke every school rule imaginable by taking out my cell phone and calling Joclyn. Luckily she answered and I gave Judy the phone. Judy said hello and told my wife she hoped she would get a new heart soon. She ended the conversation with "you are my favorite wife." I was not aware of how much my students shared with one another. By the time that Tuesday rolled around, they were all waiting for the news delivered by Mr. O.

Joclyn

Speaking of wild conspiracy theories, a doctor at Weill Cornell told me, while I was there, that the possibility exists that transplant recipients could avoid taking toxic anti-rejection medication. In this scenario, my own DNA would be injected into my transplanted heart. My body could thereby be deceived into accepting the heart as my own, eliminating the danger of rejection — and the need for anti-rejection drugs. The transplanted heart would just be, well, my heart. The issue, of course, is financing for the research. Pharmaceutical companies profit handsomely from the sale of big-ticket anti-rejection drugs. We would later learn that my medication costs approximately $8,000 per MONTH (and we pay about $100 per month in copayments). Similar to how the oil companies bought the patents to alternative energy technologies and squelched their development in the 1980s, the drug companies bought the patents to transplant drug research as well, and have chosen to sit on it. How evil is that? The medicine that keeps people's immune systems from destroying transplanted organs is itself poison, slowly damaging livers and kidneys and God knows what else over the years. In fact, these life-saving drugs may contribute to premature deaths of people who take them. A healthier alternative exists, but it doesn't produce the kinds of profits for shareholders that a lifetime prescription for some of the most expensive pharmaceutical products on the market does. In other words, a group of people with power decided that they are not quite wealthy enough and are actively prohibiting necessary research from occurring.

What a great world we live in.

Also speaking of wild conspiracy theories, or at least of not being able to trust what I read and hear, I was supposedly only given gluten-free hospital food, officially. It was so marked on the menus that would accompany the vile food trays. Sometimes alongside the maroon covered plate was a wrapped pastry or cookie, wrapped in clear cellophane and bearing no label. The menu was clear; part of my "order" included a "gluten-free cookie," but I was afraid to eat it. All of a sudden I was to trust a blank wrapper? I mean, generally the kitchen provided me with the above-mentioned Rice Chex, exquisitely labeled, but if the regular dietary workers at Weill Cornell were out that day, the Rice Chex was replaced with Cheerios (not gluten-free) and my food was served alongside regular bread. Jeremy, I think, thought I was being ridiculous at first, but as he was yanked along the rocky pavement of advocating for yourself in the hospital, he realized that it was quite possible that these cookies had nothing to do with alternate grains. "It doesn't taste very good" was not proof enough. I ate one or two of them in desperation at some point over the weeks.

To add to the food torture (possibly another conspiracy of some kind) was the constant finger sticks. Hospitalized people are all treated like diabetics. My blood sugar was checked via painful stab to the fingertip at least three times a day, and seemed to always be done immediately following a meal. Eating raises blood sugar, as does the stress of being hospitalized, as does being on corticosteroids. So, naturally, I was frequently dosed with insulin, also delivered via a painful, unwanted, subcutaneous assault. When I was later diagnosed with what turned out to be a temporary, non-hospital based brand of diabetes, no doubt one might understand my lingering skepticism, even as I traipsed from pharmacy to pharmacy very late at night on the Upper West Side of Manhattan looking, fruitlessly, for a specific type of "pen" needed to administer the specific brand of quick-acting insulin I had been incorrectly prescribed during an all-day yet hasty discharge following an emergent admission secondary to a ridiculously high blood glucose reading of 600. It may have been higher. My meter only registers up to 600. Normally, blood glucose levels for a non-diabetic are in the 70–100 range, and may go as high as 140 if checked within two hours of a meal. Seriously.

There remains at least one doctor at the Naomi Berrie Diabetes Center at Columbia, who insists on referring to me as "pre-diabetic," and another practitioner there who suggested I "may have the kind of diabetes you don't have to do anything about." Of course.

Football season was in full swing during all this, of course. While I was still in the little horse stall room of the cardiac ICU, not a full 48 hours post-transplant, the Jets were playing the Chargers in the second round of the playoffs. The Jets won, and Jeremy was nearly asked to leave when he cheered and made noise. He was nearly asked to leave several times, all for minor infractions, none of which would have been worse for me than his forced absence from my bedside.

So not only were we made to strain in discomfort while watching TV, but we also were not to audibly enjoy it. It was an intensive care unit, not a library. The sports fanaticism was a welcome distraction from the beeping (the BEEPING), and the smells, and the unreliable smiles who always promised and ultimately delivered but made me wait and wait and wait and wait and wait.

"Why do you want to brush your teeth?"

Because I can. Same goes for the cheering for the Jets. Please stop interrupting us. We are trying to live here.

Sundays are often not counted as regular business days in hospitals, and things slow down even more when followed by a holiday. So my promised transfer from ICU to a step-down unit was delayed because of Martin Luther King Day. Jeremy returned to work on the Tuesday following. Ellen offered to come in case the transfer did happen earlier in the day. "Ellen to the rescue" as we like to say now. She was able to make sure that all of my stuff followed me as it did not all fit in the space allotted by the rolling stretcher.

As the time until discharge home grew closer, the tiny TV — which followed me from ICU to step-down to My Own Room — was somewhat of a catalyst for change as well. Jeremy's insistence that "We are NOT watching the Superbowl on this tiny TV!" may have pushed my discharge date back from the Monday to the Friday.

CHAPTER 40

LUCKY LEE

Jeremy

The family visits continued as Lee arrived in town from San Diego. I was at work and he got to see Joclyn in the step-down unit before I did. He saw her with the one IV bag attached to her. He was fortunate to have never witnessed all the tubes and drainage pipes that terrified all the previous visitors. I was glad to have someone around I could run out and get a beer with. It had been a few weeks since I had pizza and beer with Matthew, so going to Coogan's for a beer and some pub food was a much-needed diversion. Lee spoke about the whole experience of the heart transplant from his perspective in California via text messages. I was reminded about the impact this ordeal had on our family and friends. Lee's visit was very nice and came at a rare time when things were going well for us. I think we all appreciated the break from drama and panic. I felt sad when Lee's visit came to an end and remember promising him that Joclyn and I would make it back to San Diego together sometime in the future.

Joclyn

After my transplant surgery Lee, Jeremy's oldest brother, flew in from San Diego to hang out with me for a few days. This was poignant beyond just what it was because before the world ended Jeremy and I had planned to spend Christmas break with he and Kathy and their kids in San Diego. Even after I first became ill and was initially diagnosed, I maintained that Jeremy and I would proceed with our plans to visit. "We're coming! We're Jews and the plane tickets are non-refundable," I insisted. When a nurse's aide, Pauline, the sole kind nursing aide at Columbia, tried to convince me to get out of bed, I protested. I hated being told what to do; I had wasted away to 100 pounds at that point, and I wanted to be left alone. Without judgment, Lee calmly asked, "Why don't you want to get up?" I got up. He brought me cinnamon oatmeal. After eating some of the oatmeal (which would last for days as I was starving but again endlessly nauseous,) it was time for my bedside physical therapy. The lesson of the day happened to be "sidestepping." I already knew how to walk sideways, obviously, but with a visiting brother-in-law from California this exercise seamlessly transitioned from counting and stepping into a fun, giggly dance! I told him that he dances better than his brother. Without Lee's visit, I would have refused to rise from bed altogether. I think Lee lucked out in terms of the timing of his visit. He didn't see me at my best, but things were certainly more positive. He's not one for blood, I hear, but really, who is?

CHAPTER 41

AIN'T GOT NO RHYTHM

Jeremy

The physical and occupational therapists' visits encouraged us greatly. For Joclyn, when she was at her sickest, walking required the help of a nurse and me, along with both therapists. We formed an entourage that would turn heads as we walked around the hospital. This practice had to be canceled when just one of the necessary members was unable to attend. After Joclyn's transplant, she only needed the assistance of one professional. I could see that Joclyn was determined to be up and walking before her discharge; she requested that we walk around the halls of the hospital for the majority of the time I was with her. We were almost at a point when walking would only require the two of us, but that was delayed when we had trouble with the external pacemaker. Joclyn's new heart was struggling to find and maintain its own rhythm. If there was no improvement, a permanent pacemaker would be necessary. I hoped we would get a break and she would be spared another dose of bad news, but we prepared for the worst.

I hoped we would have an answer soon, because Joclyn's doctors appeared uneasy. One of them named Latif feared an accident with the external pacemaker, and hinted at the need to put Joclyn back in intensive care. Joclyn was not happy about this. She took issue with Latif's cautious approach, which she believed was the opposite of what she needed, and was definitely the opposite of what gave her comfort. I understood the doctor's concern, but I could not dare to openly support Joclyn's return to the intensive care unit. Dr. Latif's concerns were proven correct when a night nurse came within inches of yanking the wires out of Joclyn's chest while trying to straighten out her blankets and sheets.

Joclyn

Since I am an occupational therapist by profession, one might expect that I would appreciate such rehabilitation services while a patient. Pre-transplant, while I was attached to the CentriMag and the LVAD, an occupational therapist (OT) and a physical therapist (PT) would come together, mostly for the practicality of moving all of the machines while I walked. It was a 3-to-4-person job, actually, so the OT, the PT, the nurse, and whichever visitor I happened to have at the moment would assist in the pushing and the holding and the encouraging. On days where I was excessively nauseous or tired, Elza the OT and Alex the PT would have me do seated exercises, which were impossibly hard for me at times. I wanted my forty pounds back. I walked as far as the main waiting room one day with their help, and this was an enormous accomplishment. Walking even the shortest distance was so difficult. Between the pain in my swollen feet from being so swollen, the muscle loss I'd experienced while bedridden, and the difficulty of taking adequate breaths because I'd had my chest opened three times by that point, endurance was hard to come by. I enjoyed PT and OT equally at that point. The high point of all of my PT/OT sessions was when I was able to finally make it all the way down the hall, around the corner, through the doors, and down another hall to the famous waiting room I'd only heard so much about. It was where guests would wait sometimes before seeing me, where Jeremy would sit with a cup of coffee or our MacBook to work on one of his graduate school assignments when someone was visiting with me, and also where my mother would sit and visit with Howie and Ellen.

Post-transplant OT was awful. I knew it would be even before it started. Just thinking about it made me seethe. "Just let some perky little shit come in here and try to explain how I should put my socks on." I don't think she even completed the evaluation, poor Whoever She Was. I never forgot how to dress myself or perform a single iota of function relating to my activities of daily living.

At Columbia, I was assigned the best PT! Her name was Sheila, and she reminded me of our good friend, also named Sheila. She was really smart, and actually taught me things that I did not already know. She showed me exercises I'd never tried before. I looked forward to her visits. When a different PT was assigned my case, though, it was ridiculous. All of the other PTs (except one young man whose name escapes me) well lived up to the stereotype that hospital-based physical therapists are merely "people-walkers." If it wasn't Sheila or this other guy, I'd walk up and down the hallway a couple of times and they would take my blood pressure and go. If I hadn't been so nauseous, I would have told them what I thought about this. I would have had Jeremy bring in one of Sedaris' leashes and I'd have handed it to them, or maybe I would have refused altogether. There was a major issue with that as a possible scenario, though. Prior to the implantation of my permanent pacemaker, I had been fitted with an external pacemaker so there were literally two wires coming from my chest and inserting themselves into a big, blue box. Because of this accouterment, it actually said somewhere in my chart that I was only to be allowed to walk with the aid of a physical therapist. Seriously? At least I come off as a smart, responsible person, and only one doctor held me to this order.

The blue box was to be held or clipped to something, and the wires were very long. The length was so absurd that it reminded me of the Bang and Olufsen headphones that Jeremy has. Yes, they sound fantastic, but the wire is so long that it is completely impossible to use them at the gym or on the subway without worrying about tripping or having to concoct some special kind of arrangement so as to make the entire operation realistic. They probably cost $300, but he somehow came into an Apple Store gift card, and had apparently been in a situation where he had to spend it on the spot. And so the headphones with the long wire, and thus my thought of them when finding myself attached to a temporary, external cardiac pacing device.

In regard to the reason why I would not have been able to refuse physical therapy even on the occasion of my session exclusively consisting of a walk up and down the hallway similar to when I used to take Sedaris out for a middle-of-the-night bathroom break. Those quick nighttime walks are where I would walk behind her, wishing I were inside, perhaps asleep, even. But had I refused, I would not have otherwise been permitted to walk outside of my room at all that day. One of the doctors, a Dr. Latif, literally made me cry over this point. She said that because my life depended on the external pacemaker wire remaining in its place unbothered, I was never to walk in the hallway by myself, not even with Jeremy, only with someone employed by Columbia University Medical Center. She may have specified that my co-walker had to be a physical therapist. Through pathetic tears, I told her that I had to walk as much as possible. I want to go home, I pleaded, and I can't even muster the gluteal strength to rise from a toilet independently. She may have said that she understood, but to this day I really don't like her. If I learn that she will be the doctor performing my outpatient biopsy and right heart catheterization, I plead with Denise the biopsy nurse (via my eyes, which she understands well) for another doctor: preferably Dr. Restaino. Dr. Restaino is the transplant cardiologist I mainly deal with; I love her touch. Dr. Latif refuses to use enough lidocaine when stabbing me in the neck to access bits of my heart for study. Dr. Latif, along with someone else on the team who clearly also isn't a psychiatrist, also wanted to move me BACK to the ICU from the step-down unit. They were so concerned that my external pacemaker would accidentally be pulled out, so they thought it would somehow aid in my recovery to put me on a unit without actual, reliable visiting hours or a place to move, or a bathroom. The cardiac ICU at Columbia is not for conscious people. It is meant for convalescence and medical monitoring post-surgical recovery while intubated and sedated. The lack of amenities and dignities prove I am correct, and it is a good thing that I was only informed of this as having been a possibility after the time in question had passed. The staff who wanted patients of the Yes, Doctor, variety would argue that I had long since unsubscribed from Being a Good Patient. I do believe that I would not have readily accepted the news of my transfer with open arms. I like to imagine that I would have warranted a call to security, even though those types of situations rarely end well, with a turn of events in the disturbed individual's favor. I am so exhausted from the state of being so powerless, then and now.

CHAPTER 42

JUST A YANK

Jeremy

Of course nothing ever came easily to us, especially in this period of our lives. So, I was not surprised when one of the nurses told us that Joclyn would need a pacemaker installed permanently to help her new heart maintain a steady beat. In fact, this isn't as serious as it sounds, and it doesn't imply there are any problems with Joclyn's new heart. It was not uncommon. As Joclyn loves to remind me, however, if I needed a pacemaker installed it would represent a medical crisis for me. And she would be correct. But at this point, I was just happy to have my wife back without seeing her hooked to huge machines with huge tubes going in and out of her. The procedure was easy for me: I came to the hospital from work and was told it was done. For Joclyn, it was another invasion of her body that provided her a day of discomfort. The only thing that made it bearable was that Ellen came in and stayed with her the whole time. It was not the first or the last time Ellen saved the day.

Joclyn

When I think of it now, resultant chest tube aside, the placement of the permanent pacemaker in lieu of the external, precarious one was really a great thing. I finally understood that I definitely required a permanently implanted pacemaker when a resident momentarily unplugged the external one. I remember that the room quickly faded, and I whispered an "I don't feel well."

It meant that I was now self-contained. I was free to walk around and redevelop my muscles. Of course, once the team realized that one of my lungs had partially collapsed, I was then bogged down with a giant chest tube drainage system, and also required to occasionally attach to the wall heart monitor, confining me not only to my room, but also to bed.

The difference was an immediate relief. I was dismayed to learn that the external pacing wires would not be removed during the spooky-awake-pacemaker-placement surgery in which I could hear the banter of the surgeons, including the super-comforting "This is always so tricky with the transplant patients!" During this procedure, I was able to convince a caring surgical nurse to free my right arm from the "sterile field," the areas during surgery that must be protected from germs with gloves and gowns. A continuing effect of an earlier arterial line placement in my wrist (a common alternative to regular intravenous therapy with ICU patients) was that the entire inside surface of my forearm had bruised purple and I was unable to turn my palm back and forth. She was kind enough to let me move my arm into a more comfortable position so it wouldn't throb with numbness.

"You're leaving those in?" pointing to the dangly wires, my eyes pleading for sympathy from the same nurse who freed my arm.

"Oh, yes. The team on the floor will remove them."

This couldn't have been coordinated? Ever since the CentriMag and LVAD ceased to dangle from my chest, I'd preferred a life of disentanglement from such devices. I'd have always preferred such a state even prior to this pickle. I'd never even have thought it up, though, let alone had the ability to not wish it for myself.

Of course, when the time came for the external pacing wires to be removed, it turned out that the process is nothing more than a simple yanking. Seriously. A resident presented this to me in the same way as was every other horrific procedure done outside the sterility of an operating room. Someone announced from either the doorway or the foot of my bed that such-and-such would be performed today; I would look over at the clock and note that it was 6:00 am. I would have the whole day to nervously ruminate. Twelve hours later, just in time to ruin my visit with Jeremy, a doctor would come in and dispatch with whatever was on the medical menu for the day.

So at some point, probably about two days and fourteen hours beyond when I was told that it would happen, a resident came in and yanked out my now detached external pacing wires. This is my memory, but I feel like it can't actually be what happened, because weren't those wires anchored into my new heart somehow? I don't remember my chest or any other usually-closed section of my body being reopened ever while not under at least local anesthesia. So, I know that the wires were not surgically removed, and the only things I remember snipped with scissors and left to auto-amputate were various stitches holding closed some key surgical wounds. The only thing really left, I imagine, was the possibility that the now-defunct wires were yanked from my chest, probably in time with a command to hold my breath and then "forcefully let it out, yeah!" This was an exact recreation of the chest tube extraction, which, while similar to what is described above, doesn't make my nose scrunch up in distaste or my throat close in fearful nausea.

Or is it more accurate to say that chest tube extraction is an exact recreation of pacer wire extraction? It's a chicken or egg, who predates what kind of question, really, because I actually had several chest tube extractions prior to the one that was done to me while conscious and miserable, as opposed to actively dying and asleep in surgery. No dead horse beating, but would it become less upsetting to recall if one happened first rather than the other? I could also say that the removal of my umbilicus after being born was a similar procedure to the auto-falling-out process foisted onto me and the stitches that were left to fall out on their own.

CHAPTER 43

A LUNG PIERCING

Jeremy

Just when I thought we could count down the days till I took Joclyn home, she started to experience discomfort in her breathing. When doctors install a pacemaker, they warn the patient that there is a small chance, during the procedure, that they will puncture a lung. Should we have been surprised that this would happen to Joclyn? Now she needed to have a tube put into her lung to reflate it. The tube was attached to a machine that sent in the air. It would have to stay in until her lung was back to normal. The procedure to put it in was very painful, and I almost passed out watching my wife experience more pain and suffering. It took a long time for the doctor to get the tube right and Joclyn was in so much pain she cried. I was shaking. Eventually, the doctor finished the procedure, and the pain slowly faded. We were frustrated because this was another delay that would keep her in the hospital. Joclyn understandably asked me, "When will this end?" I promised her we would be home for the Superbowl.

After a few days of discomfort, the device blowing air into Joclyn's lungs was finally removed. It appeared her breathing was back to normal. The only obstacle now to Joclyn's return home was getting her medication doses correct. One of the key medications that prevents rejection is called Prograf. The desired level of Prograf in the blood is about 12. They called this the "Goldilocks." Joclyn kept bouncing around from 6, then to 20. This was too important to ignore, and the amount of Prograf she took each day kept changing. We were also being trained and educated on all of the other medications. As the individual responsible for setting up her medication each day, I made it a point to pay close attention and start remembering all the names of the medications. It was a lot. We would eventually need an entire cabinet dedicated to all of Joclyn's medication. Each time a blood test came back the Prograf level was off. I began to despise the term "Goldilocks."

Joclyn

The introduction of the idea of a chest tube was pretty horrific. I was bumming around in my private, river-facing room at Columbia, enjoying the impression that I would go home in a few days. Emerging from the bathroom, a woman whom I'd never seen before was placing a gigantic, Fischer-Price-looking container on the floor, just inside the doorway to my room.

"What is that?"

"It's for your chest tube."

"I don't have a chest tube."

I thought I saw a smile encroaching upon her prematurely-aging face. "You'd better talk to the doctor. They just told me to put this here."

After the multiple surgeries and trauma, I really did not know how much more I could endure. I had already been given a tentative date to go home and resume cohabitation with Jeremy and Sedaris. Chest tubes also really are incredibly painful going in, as I'd often heard. I recalled a bike accident my father suffered when I was very young, after which he'd needed a chest tube for a collapsed lung. Even though I'd been very small, I was able to recount almost his entire description of how they cut into his chest using a pretty large scalpel and only a tiny amount of local anesthesia.

I may have started to cry. I called for my nurse via the call bell, frustratingly aware that the person answering could not hear me. As usual, as my voice had all but vanished into a raspy whisper, and even though Nyree the transplant nurse had supposedly "put a note," the unit clerks would invariably repeat the "Can I Help You" query over and over, before angrily hanging up and sending a nurse in. I knew they'd send the nurse in.

Lissy the nurse came in. "Miss Joclyn, just don't worry" she accented. Sensing my worry, she moved the chest tube collection box from my room. I didn't actually believe that this could mean that I would not, in fact, be having a chest tube stabbed into me while awake. You may have noticed that things hadn't really been working out for me lately.

A doctor whose name escapes me but was young, female, Asian, and confident came in to announce that she would be inserting my chest tube. It seems as though during the pacemaker procedure, one of the scary things that was listed as a possible "side effect" came true. I'd developed a partially collapsed lung, and frankly this did not surprise me. Rare side effects almost behoove me, or at least they think they do, or they would if side effects thought about things. Maybe they like how I handle them. I had noticed that gradually over the two preceding days, whenever I went to the bathroom I would feel and hear a crinkling plastic bag sound in my chest. Apparently, that was the sound of a partially collapsed lung. Why couldn't the pacemaker surgeon have been more careful? Remembering that I'd overheard an "Oh, this is always so much more difficult in the transplant patients" made me briefly consider a malpractice litigation event, but who can even think about lawsuits when intercostal puncture is imminent?

I begged that the procedure be postponed until Jeremy arrived from work. This was more than I thought I could bear. I wanted a discharge date that stuck, already. Jeremy always arrived in my room about an hour after telling me he was getting on the subway. I promised the doctors who were now frequently reappearing in earnest that I would cooperate when my husband arrived.

When Jeremy did arrive, everyone made themselves scarce, it seemed. He became upset with me for having delayed the process. "You should have just let them do it." Growing impatient, I probably cried again. I felt like saying that he wouldn't be able to live my life for even ten minutes at that point. That would have felt mean afterwards.

I'm not sure why lidocaine was used. It presents a guise of anesthesia, but the part that hurts is when the tube pushes through the intercostal muscle and pierces the lung. The stinging on the skin hardly seems to be an issue once the former is faced. I looked at Jeremy. I may have held his hand. God bless him.

"I'm sorry" as I yelled in pain. I honestly, desperately, did not know how much more I could take.

Oh, no, but there was plenty more to take as the part that follows chest tube insertion is the attachment of the outer tube to the Fischer-Price-appearing box, which has a suction attachment that hooks to a spigot on the wall. Combine that with the external pacemaker wires to which I was still attached, even though the permanent pacemaker had been implanted (partially collapsing one of my lungs), plus the weight of the box and the trip hazard of all the goddamn tubes and wires, and I was pretty much bedridden — again. Call me a basket case, for that I was. As usual, I was the only one who outwardly was displeased with being told to remain bedbound. By making it an issue, I was forced to obsess over toileting.

How will I go to the bathroom? Going to the bathroom was now the most important part of my day. I went often, alone, and did not want this privilege stripped yet again.

CHAPTER 44

DANGER: STREET MEAT AHEAD

Jeremy

The Jets lost to the Colts and we were nearing the Superbowl. It was only a week away. Joclyn's team would promise us a discharge date, only to push it back because they couldn't quite get her Prograf level to 12, or maintain it at that level for a sufficient duration. Joclyn was still taking medication for nausea. We began to wonder if that would ever cease to be an issue as well. It was Saturday night; I went outside and grabbed a sausage and pepper sandwich from the street cart. As I ate it Joclyn warned me that I should avoid "street meat." I reminded her that I had an iron stomach and ate it happily. Unfortunately my iron stomach was not what it once was, and I was in the bathroom throwing up a couple of hours later. I pulled out the chair that converted to a sorry excuse for a bed and covered myself with a blanket falling asleep to the sound of Joclyn telling me "I told you so."

It turns out I was sick. I had a fever. When I woke up the next morning, the nurses told me I would have to leave. Joclyn could not be near me when I was sick because it would put her in danger. Joclyn was upset that I had to leave, but also worried about me and wanted me to hurry home to rest. We were approaching Joclyn's discharge date. We didn't need her contracting the flu from me. So, I took the train home. Joclyn's doctors continued to work at establishing an adequate level of medication in her system, and then sustaining it there. I spent two days in bed unable to hold down food. I was more upset about Joclyn being alone in the hospital.

Finally, I was able to eat half a bagel with smoked salmon cream cheese that our neighbor Brendan was kind enough to pick up for me. Marc had also dropped off soup and some other treats for me. Now that I was holding down food and the fever had broken, I was able to return to work, and then to the hospital to see Joclyn.

When I returned to the hospital, Nyree the transplant coordinator visited Joclyn and me to continue the tutorial on Joclyn's medications. She presented us with a three-month supply of medication which consisted of a shopping bag full of bottles. I wondered how we were going to figure it all out and make sure she took all of her medication on schedule each day. I learned to use weekly pill organizers, which relieved me of some of the anxiety I felt around this complex array of pills and prescriptions. I began a process which I have followed for years; I was the lucky guy who volunteered to accept responsibility for organizing and maintaining Joclyn's prescriptions. As it turns out, I am really good at it. Knowing that I am the keeper of the organizers actually relaxes me, because I know the doses and times are arranged properly. My father was a pharmacist before he partnered in the surgical supply business. Maybe counting pills was in my genes.

Joclyn

Assistant Dr. So-and-So, who hung out with the rheumatologist from Weill Cornell came to visit me at Columbia, mainly to obtain my consent to study my (native) heart, but also to tell me that I got the heart in the "nick" of time. Seriously, she told me that I would not have lived another week. I believed her and I hated her all at once. She also reminded me that there was a strong likelihood of the giant cell returning. I finally asked her what the whole point of my transplant was. She shrugged. Seriously?

I enjoy every time I retell this tidbit to someone who knows, and they tell me in their own objective way what a complete idiot she is. The doctors at Weill Cornell had told Jeremy that they had no idea how long the machines could have kept me alive. She was inaccurate in estimating that I had had less than a week to live. In fact, she was wildly off-base. I don't wonder about her anymore, and I do think I would tell her off in some sort of way if I saw her again. She upset me, and while all of this upset me, she was wrong about it after all, and therefore caused me unnecessary anguish.

Jeremy occasionally spent the night on a chair that fully reclined. One of those nights ended sadly, when he became violently sick. He either had the flu, or ate some bad street meat, which I had warned him against. Following an entire overnight of vomiting and shivering, Jeremy left at sunrise, right after a nurse came in and asked why I was wearing a mask. I asked the nurse for a Tylenol and slipped it to him. To this day, neither of us can even smell street meat (food from poorly regulated food carts. See also: dirty water dogs) without our stomachs clenching in pre-emptive nausea. I really didn't want him to go home, but I also didn't want to come down with whatever it was that made him sick. Because I was new to the issue of immunosuppression, I really wasn't ready to start taking chances — which could, at a minimum, extend my hospital stay because of some opportunistic infection. That is what they call things that can kill someone with my clinical issues, but that only send people like Jeremy to bed for a day or two.

Jeremy left, and our relationship was reduced to infrequent text messages over the course of the next 36 hours or so with neither of us able to care, tangibly, for the other. Not that I would have been able to do much for him had he stayed in the hospital. Our neighbor Brendan brought him bagels with lox cream cheese and Gatorade, and my father dropped off hot and sour soup and greasy Chinese appetizers, so at least he was sustained food-wise. But I really was at a loss for how to conduct myself in his indefinite absence. What if he had the flu? That could have put my hospital room off-limits to him for a week, and that really would have been a thing for me to deal with, emotionally. My BlackBerry lifeline pinged me with updates like "sleeping, sort of" or "watching TV" or "just threw up." I panicked a bit when Jeremy stayed home from work the following day, still unsure of the duration of this separation.

When he gave word of his recovery, I was thrilled, but also worried about the lost time. He had several papers to complete for his graduate education courses, and often worked on them while visiting me. I worried that the loss of a day might mean even more time away from me. Somehow, in his supreme ability to really just be there for me 100%, he fell right back into our miserable routine of nightly visits, and essentially full-weekend visits. He would even sleep over a few times after that. Post-transplant, as I was more mobile than before, I did actually regularly leave my bed to use the toilet. It was a bit of a throwback to Sisyphus, especially when attached to the chest tube vac machine. My quadriceps were not strong enough to assist much in the hoist from off of the low toilet in my bathroom, so I used a bedside commode that had been raised to its highest level. I was essentially standing while using it. It was a pathetic throne that required, but did not offer, privacy.

Because of this improvement, I no longer had the dread of Jeremy being in the room while I used a bedpan; instead, he was in the room while I sat on a toilet. I needed him to assist with finagling all of my wires and attachments and external pacing wires when I moved between the bed and the throne, though, and this was a new and different stressor. Terrific.

The commode equally annoyed the nursing assistants who were assigned to me.

"Why don't you just use the bathroom?" they asked without waiting for the explanation.

I would have told them that I wasn't strong enough to stand up from a regular toilet, and also wasn't strong enough psychologically to patiently wait the 35 minutes for someone to come to help me up if I tried and failed. I understand that they didn't want to empty a potty, but maybe hospital work wasn't their forte either. I was easy. I was young. I didn't scream and moan and cry and go to the bathroom ON myself. Training wouldn't have helped. People are people.

The throne commode that stood next to my bed taunted me. The nursing assistants (who were largely the antithesis of pretty much anyone who had worked with me at Weill Cornell) must have thought I had some nerve to want raw urine and feces removed from my bedside, huh? Hygiene-wise, Columbia is also the antithesis of my Weill Cornell bathing experience. The nursing assistants had never bothered to educate themselves on the wasting of muscle which occurs in the bedridden patient. One of them in particular didn't seem to be much of a people person, as it turned out. She couldn't possibly understand that while I could get myself to the bathroom, the low height of the toilet seat made it pretty much impossible for me to stand up from it independently. It was even difficult with assistance. Instead of thinking about the fact that this must be very upsetting to me, as rising from a toilet had never been something which I'd needed to think about before, she acted as if I were stupid and lazy, to have eyes rolled at, and to be offered no patience. At the time, I loathed her. She played the same role as some of those who took such excellent care of me at the other hospital, and yet seemed so hateful. Now, looking back, I feel pity for her.

I did have the fortune of being assigned one extremely kind nursing aide at Columbia. Her name was Pauline, and she visited me frequently, usually to braid my hair and put some kind of itch-minimizing wax in it. She made me feel like I was almost in a salon, gossiping about celebrities and asking me questions about Jeremy. Naturally, she was quickly reassigned to the psych unit, and so I did not see any of her after that.

CHAPTER 45

HOMEWARD BOUND

Jeremy

On a Friday just two days before the Superbowl, Joclyn's doctors finally told us that her medication levels had finally stabilized, and that she could come home with me the next day. I was excited, thrilled, and nervous all at the same time. I was worried about Joclyn's continued nausea as well. They had not been able to solve that problem, and the thought of her throwing up her meds at home scared me. Keeping the correct level of medication in her blood is what kept her immune system from rejecting her new heart. She was also taking medication to help prevent the return of the autoimmune disease that got us in this mess. It was bad enough that statistics suggested there was a 25% chance it would return even if we did everything right. At the same time, I was tiring of the hospital and was excited at the thought of going home and perhaps returning to normalcy.

The next morning, I drove to the hospital and put my car in the hospital parking lot. I went upstairs and Joclyn and I began the two-hour process of getting the hell out of there. It seemed like eight hours, and I kept getting texts and emails asking if we were home yet. I promised everyone I would let them know as soon as we walked through the front door. After the IV was removed from Joclyn's arm, she signed her discharge papers. We headed down to the lobby with our belongings. My heart was pounding with excitement. It had been a little over nine weeks since Joclyn had been home, and it seemed like a lifetime. We did not know what our lives were going to be like moving forward, but we both believed we had survived the worst of it.

I went to the parking window and gave in my ticket and was told the car would be ready in a few minutes. Joclyn was staring outside, and looking around at the lobby with big wide-open eyes. It had been so long since she was dressed in regular clothing and surrounded by the hustle and bustle of New York City life. The car finally arrived. Before I knew it we were heading down the West Side Highway towards Brooklyn. Joclyn had tears in her eyes and kept saying how beautiful everything was, and how much she had taken the city for granted before all this happened. I drove carefully thinking the last thing I wanted was anything to get in the way of getting her home safely. There was no traffic and it was not long before we were heading through the Battery Tunnel. I pulled into the driveway. My heart was pounding even harder. Joclyn was trembling. I understood why.

Joclyn

I was thrilled to return home. Hearing from one of my doctors that "just because you are going home it doesn't mean you won't be back" was a bit more than I could handle, so I chose not to.

Tempering the joy in the days leading up to going home was nausea with a capital "N." I was completely on the verge of vomiting pretty much since I first set foot in the hospital. I couldn't take my anti-rejection medications unless I had been given Zofran or Reglan or I would puke them up, intact, into that damned pink basin. Both of those medications had been administered intravenously. The medical staff assured me that oral versions of both those medications exist. I was promised a prescription. I was cautioned not to take too much. I told myself I would take too much. That had to be a better option than throwing up the anti-rejection meds and dying from rejection. Everyone thinks they are so smart. It turned out that going home would be the ultimate antiemetic.

Many people asked if my new heart made me feel different.

"Do you like any new foods?"

I've since met a girl who insists that she'd always hated apple pie. After her heart transplant, she says, she changed course completely and now requests it exclusively when offered dessert.

I still like most foods, and haven't noticed any significant change in my preferences.

"Do you still love Jeremy?"

The heart was seemingly first used to symbolize love in the year 1250, in the French romance *Roman de la poire*. Ahead of his time, the lover in the tale is depicted handing his heart to his lady friend. He didn't give her a grotesque, bloody organ and then die, of course. He gave her what looked sort of like an upside-down pine cone, and she appeared pleased and smitten. This pinecone image of love and devotion reappeared many times through the art ages both as a gift to lovers and an offering to God. Around the 15th Century, the pinecone shape evolved into the more familiar playing card-style heart symbol. The gift of such has an unmistakable intent.

Jeremy, during our ordeal, had an unmistakable intent. He gave me all of his energy, all of his time, all of his love, all of his wants, all. He would have traded places with me if he could have. I don't know if I would have let him. He would have insisted. I was nothing without him. I couldn't breathe. I couldn't swallow. I was a real person with him.

Someone asked, someone really, actually asked if I still loved Jeremy. She was probably just making conversation, believing what she once read somewhere about people waking up from organ transplant surgery with new accents and strange preferences. My damaged heart was gone, but my new heart was bursting. It was bursting with the promise of health, longevity, and a return to normalcy. But things would never be normal. My appreciation, and of course my unwavering love for my husband had swollen to unimaginable depths, even still. Unimaginable.

From the Post, or After, frame of reference, I have been out of work, disabled, so to speak, at least legally. I am in my early thirties and a licensed and registered occupational therapist with flexibility of skills, as evidenced by my resume and LinkedIn recommendations. Prior to my return to work, I had not logged into monster.com in over two years. Yet I continued to receive job

JOCLYN AND JEREMY KREVAT

offers, via email and phone, almost daily, even while still in the hospital. I could not accept any of them, or even respond really, although that part is mainly out of embarrassment. Psychologically, or maybe it is intuitively, I feel like there must have been something I did to bring this rare and fatal illness on myself. Or that I at least should have seen it coming and been somehow able to prevent it, or mitigate it somehow. Jeremy and I had just gotten married, after all, and the two of us combined were making pretty good money. The housing market was in our favor. We'd put in an offer. Several, actually. I think on one we had been outbid by only $5,000. Disappointing at the time, had any of our offers been accepted, we'd have had to walk away due to the subsequent and catastrophic health events that followed. Alive People Problems.

I do keep searching back in my mind, seeking an explanation or some kind of reasoning for what happened to me, to us. I continue to think that it isn't fair, but I know that the universe cares not for that type of hypothesizing. I enjoy crediting the DVD player with the arrival of my heart, though. I enjoy crediting the prayer circles. I enjoy crediting that Jeremy and I had just recently wed, and for me to die would have just been out of hand, unfair to him. I particularly enjoy crediting my donor, without whom, really, certainly I would not have made it through. I mean, I imagine I would have likely received a different person's heart, but this one seems to be working out well.

CHAPTER 46

TUNA SANDWICH?

Jeremy

When we were in the house Joclyn told me she was hungry and asked for a tuna fish sandwich. I quickly made her one. I was glad she had an appetite. I expected her to eat half of it, then complain about the usual nausea that followed every time she ate. Joclyn did not return half the sandwich; she asked me for another one. I happily made her another one and she ate it without any nausea at all. We did not want to jinx anything, so we turned on the TV and relaxed. In a few minutes, I got up and headed to the office in the back of our apartment. I logged on to the CaringBridge website and posted the last entry I would make in several months: "Joclyn is home!"

Acknowledgments

We need to thank so many. First, to the physicians who saved Joclyn's life, Drs. Bender, Chen, Horn, Ghaly, and Williams, thank you for your brilliant minds and dexterous hands. Thank you to the critical care nurses and to everyone at the New York–Presbyterian Hospital network who helped us survive.

Our families inspired us to live rather than merely survive through our ordeal:

Manny and Sandra Krevat, Matthew and Madhavi Krevat, Lee and Kathy Krevat, Marc Gordon and Cheryl Zellman, Jay and Leslie Altman, Rachel Gordon, Susan and Michael Friedman, Robin Friedman and Declan Spring, Andrew Friedman and Adriana Villegas.

A thank you will never be enough for our friends who showed up and then some:

Melissa and Austin Harclerode (for EVERYTHING, especially for taking loving care of sweet Sedaris), Mo and Charlene Goldner, John and Maria Lennon, Stan and Eileen Goldner, Howard, Ellen, and Carrie Margulies, Heather and Jason Bergman, Jack and Lori Falzone, David and Danielle Falzone, Leon and Marion Rumsky, John and Martina Gibilaro, Frank Grasso and Jenny Basil, Faith and Gabriel DiAngelis, Mara Levine, Rebecca Ostro Nagata, Andy and Arleen Meppen, Mike Marty, Zachary Hayes, Melissa Schaeffer, Jena Corsello, Glen Gillen, Janet Falk-Kessler, Kyle Fitzpatrick, Kristen Ryan, Mark Lesser, Nora Byrd, Jeffrey Uslip, and the late (and sorely missed) Tom Hughes.

Special thanks to David Sedaris for his (now printed out and autographed) email. A funny email is a priceless gem in the ICU.

Maybe we are unlucky. But see how lucky we are.

Sweet Sedaris
Prospect Park, Brooklyn, New York

Made in the USA
Middletown, DE
08 September 2018